# What the world's leading author of business best-sellers is saying about The One Page Business Plan®...

"The One Page Business Plan is an out-and-out winner. Period.

It makes great sense to me as a so-called *business thinker*. But the acid test was applying it to a start-up I co-founded. We spent several days drafting our one pager — and have been editing it ever since. It is a powerful, living document; the very nature of which has led us to important new insights.

The One Page Business Plan = the proverbial better mouse trap!"

## — Tom Peters

author of
*In Search of Excellence,*
*Thriving on Chaos,*
*Liberation Management,*
*The Pursuit of Wow!,*
and *The Circle of Innovation*

D1557827

WARNING — DISCLAIMER

This book was designed to provide information in regard to the subject matter covered. It is not the purpose of this manual to reprint all of the information available to the author/publisher, but to complement, amplify and supplement other sources.

Use of The One Page Business Plan® does not in any way guarantee the success of an idea or organization, nor does it ensure that financing will be made available. When legal or expert assistance is required, the services of a competent professional should be sought.

The author/publisher shall have neither liability nor responsibility to any person or entity with respect to any loss or damage caused, or alleged to be caused, directly or indirectly by the information contained in this book.

**If you do not wish to be bound by the above, you may return this book to the publisher for a full refund.**

Published by:

**The One Page**  **Business Plan® Company**

1798 Fifth Street
Berkeley, CA 94710
Phone: (510) 705-8400
Fax:  (510) 705-8403
e-mail: jhoran@onepagebusinessplan.com
www.onepagebusinessplan.com

6th Printing 2004, Third Edition with CD-ROM

ISBN: 1-891315-09-9

Book design by Designwise™
Edited by Rebecca Salome Shaw, Entrepreneurial Authors
Printed in the United States of America

# The One Page Business Plan®

*Start with a vision, build a company!*

by

Jim Horan

# What Others Are Saying

**The One Page Business Plan® takes a complex process and makes it simple!**

"I've had a number of business plans, but none of them were effective. Having all the essentials of our plan on one page helped get me and my partners on track!"

**Norman Kurtin, Design Media, Inc.**

"The friendly visual graphics, and the no-nonsense approach to business planning got me over my reluctance to write a business plan. This process got me to think out of the box and to create my dream business! Now I have a great plan and it's working."

**Kendall Moalem, Kendall Moalem Design**

"My board of advisors applauded my one page business plan. They finally understood my business and are contributing important advice because they have a written plan to review."

**Nicole Lazzaro, President, XEODesign, Inc.**

"I was too busy developing plans for clients to complete my own, but a one page business plan of key words and short phrases seemed so easy and "doable" that I wrote one immediately!"

**Diane Weinsheimer, The Marketing Manager**

"I have been writing the same goals and visions for my business over and over. What I wrote in March, I wrote in June, and again in September. After I heard Jim speak, I wrote my one page plan. I now choose my opportunities more wisely and waste less time because I have my plan in place."

**Linda Pollock, Professional Organizer**

"The One Page Business Plan is the business owner's Cliff Notes."

**Fred DaMert, Chairman, DaMert Company**

"This is an innovative, fresh approach to business planning. If all loan applicants would provide us with clear, concise summaries of their business plan, a banker's life would be a lot easier."

**Jim Ryan, Chairman, Bank of Walnut Creek, California**

"As a banker, I love The One Page Business Plan. I know the potential business owner is serious, committed and professional. This is truly a breakthrough in business planning!"

**Jerry Ricketts, Vice President, Scotts Valley Bank**

"The One Page Business Plan truly helps the prospective entrepreneur or existing business owner get focused and clear on one page. When they are clear on one page, they have a much better chance for success!"

**Greg Garrett, Program Manager, One Stop Capital Shop**

"It's easy for a stockbroker to get wrapped up in the market and lose perspective that you are in business for yourself. In order to be successful for the long run, one must have a plan and The One Page Business Plan is a great tool."

**Ralph Miljanich, Vice President, Dean Witter Reynolds, Inc.**

"It's wonderful that someone finally came up with a business plan for independent professionals. It de-mystifies business planning so that the average business professional can actually write a business plan that makes sense!"

**Rebecca Salome Shaw, Entrepreneurial Authors**

"The One Page Business Plan revolutionizes business planning! It cuts the fluff and the filler and gets right to the point. This is a powerful tool for businesses of all sizes!"

**Roger McAniff, Sage Consulting**

*This book is dedicated to the*
*family, friends, and the extended*
*community that supports and*
*nurtures entrepreneurs.*

*Without their love and support,*
*many entrepreneurs would not be able to*
*make their dreams come true.*

**Introducing**

# The One Page Business Plan®

---

## Colorado Garden Window Company
### 2004 Business Plan Summary

vision

> Become recognized as the leader in designing and manufacturing custom and replacement garden windows and skylights.

mission

> Bring light, air and the beauty of nature into homes through creative windows!

objectives

Achieve 2004 sales of $17 million with $1.5 million in pretax profits.
Grow garden window division at 8% per year and achieve $5.3 million in 2004.
Expand skylight/custom window product lines; grow sales to $7.5 million in 2004.
Implement profit improvement programs & reduce product cost to 38%.
Reduce distribution costs to 4% of sales thru facility consolidation & technology.
Reduce inventory levels to 3.3 months by August 31st.
Achieve 98% ontime delivery with 98% order accuracy in 1st quarter.

strategies

Focus on new upscale home developments & baby-boomer remodeling trends.
Build Colorado Garden Window into nationally-recognized brand name.
Become vendor-of-choice by maintaining inventory of standard window sizes.
Control quality by manufacturing in-house.
Increase capacity by minimizing duplicate products & increasing mfg. efficiencies.
Centralize distribution into one location; reducing costs, improving service.

plans

Introduce new Scenic Garden Windows at SF Products Show (March 2004).
Hire new sales rep by April; focus on Signature Homes in Denver and Provo.
Implement new MRP software by July 31st to achieve inventory reduction.
Complete skylight product rationalization program by Aug. 15th.
Phase in new packaging design beginning March 31st.
Complete employee benefit program redesign by Sept. 30th.

**Vision**
What are you building?

**Mission**
Why does this business exist?

**Objectives**
What will you measure?

**Strategies**
How will this business be built?

**Plans**
What is the work to be done?

# Author's Note

"You must simplify.

You must make the complex simple, then you must make it work."

— I.M. Pei
Master Architect

There is a new breed of business owner in the marketplace today. These business owners are either starting up new businesses or reinventing established businesses. These individuals are intensely passionate and strategic. They are very competitive and heartfull. They care about people, the environment, and their communities. They do not run their businesses casually. They are professional entrepreneurs.

There is also another type of entrepreneur, the accidental entrepreneur. These individuals are finding themselves considering self-employment for the first time in their lives. Many have experienced firsthand the downsizing of corporate America and are now ready to act on their own business ideas.

I know the accidental entrepreneur very well, I happen to be one. I came kicking and screaming into the world of entrepreneurship in 1990 after spending 17 years in Fortune 500 companies as a senior financial executive. In 1990, I began a search for my next career. I found myself self-employed, as a business and financial advisor, drawn to working with entrepreneurs and independent business owners.

Today, Rent.a.CFO℠ is a broad-based consulting practice serving both professional and accidental entrepreneurs. Client companies are in a wide range of industries including specialty gifts, home improvement, professional services, and food products.

All these companies share similar issues. Business is complex, resources are limited, and time is of the essence. There is no room for big mistakes. Business owners can't know it all and can't do it all by themselves. Therefore, other people will become involved in the business. That means employees, independent contractors, investors, and potentially partners. Additionally, your business may require the use of "other people's money." Other people and "other people's money" necessitate having a written business plan. It's no longer optional.

The One Page Business Plan® was inspired by my work with entrepreneurs. These individuals like to think fast and move fast, and the concept of a traditional business plan was out of the question. An innovative, fresh approach to business planning was required, and the One Page Business Plan® was born.

The One Page Business Plan® is designed to act as a catalyst for your ideas. It's a powerful tool for building and managing a business in the 21st century. It's short, it's concise, and it delivers your plan quickly and effectively. There can be no question as to where you are going when it's in writing. Start with your vision, build a company.

– Jim Horan

# How to Use This Book

**The primary purpose of this book is to help you get your business plan onto paper. It has been carefully crafted to capture the business plan that is in your head.**

**Carry this book with you, write in it, use it as a container for capturing your thoughts as they occur. If you have multiple businesses, buy a book for each one.**

**It's not necessary to do all the exercises in this book. If you can write your One Page Business Plan® by reviewing the samples — skip the exercises. They are there to help guide you through the process if you need help.**

This book does not look like the typical business planning book – it isn't intended to. The exercises and examples are meant to stimulate you. The graphics and images are meant to guide you. If they look playful, be playful and explore. If they look analytical, be analytical and focused. The examples and samples are from real business plans. They are meant to show you how powerful a few words or a well-constructed phrase can be.

Not all people think or work the same way. Some are auditory; others respond visually; some need to write. Some do their best thinking alone, silently. Others do their best thinking out loud. This book has been designed to accommodate all of these different styles.

Do not underestimate the power of the questions in this book that appear simple! They are simple by design. That's so you will understand them. If you do not get an "aha" from them, have somebody ask you the questions. Important insights may begin to flow.

This book is divided into seven sections with the focus on the five elements of The One Page Business Plan®. You can start anywhere. It's OK to jump around!

There are five types of exercises in the book. They are clearly marked and identified at the top of each page. Each type of exercise is designed to achieve a specific purpose:

- **Brainstorming** – generate new ideas by considering provocative questions
- **Research** – gather information from external sources
- **Focusing** – process of prioritizing ideas and concepts
- **Summarizing** – condensing, final prioritizing, editing
- **Feedback** – solicit objective feedback from trusted advisors

There are many different ways to use and interact with this book. Exercises can be done:

- by oneself
- with a planning partner (one business owner working with another business owner)
- as a management team
- as a group – feedback exercise (one business owner receiving input from several business owners or professionals)
- by a group of entrepreneurs or business owners for brainstorming business planning concepts, ideas, strategies
- with a professional business consultant

*Some final thoughts...*

There is no right, wrong, or perfect business plan. Your business will always be evolving. So will your plan. It will also get better with time. Remember, it is not necessary to do all the exercises in this book nor is it desirable to do it all by yourself. Use this book as a catalyst. When you think you are finished, stop. If you get stuck, put it aside for a few days or a week. Come back to it when the ideas start to flow. Take your time and enjoy the journey.

# How to Use the CD

The Entrepreneur's Toolkit CD contains additional tools to make the creation of your business plan simple and easy.

The interactive exercises, forms and templates from the book are available on Microsoft Word® for those who prefer to use word processing software.

Need help estimating or budgeting your sales? The Sales Calculators on this CD are easy to use.

Budgeting? We have simplified budgeting to a single page.

Ready to track results? Use The One Page Performance Scorecards.

CD also contains ten (10) Bonus Tools and fifteen (15) additional sample plans!

## What's on your CD:

### Interactive Exercises & Templates

Included on the CD are 22 exercises from the book*. The file names on the CD relate to the specific pages in the book so they are easy to find.

Most of the forms, templates and exercises have text boxes that you can type directly into.

### Powerful Sales Calculators

Contained in your CD Toolkit are three (3) Sales Calculators* that allow you to perform multiple "what-if sales scenarios". You don't need to be a CPA, MBA, or Marketing Guru to get a sense of what your sales might look like in 1, 3, or 5 years.

Each Sales Calculator has one or more colorful, easy-to-read graphs to help you visualize the growth of your business in addition to seeing the actual numbers. This is a great tool for entrepreneurs who have been intimated by the "numbers" associated with business!

Also included with the Sales Calculators is a Sales Budgeting System that helps you create a Sales Budget by Month for up to seven products, services, product lines or business units.

* Requires Microsoft Word® and/or Excel®

## One Page Budget Worksheet

Every business needs a budget; especially small ones! Start the process by using one of the Sales Calculators to determine your sales by month, when finished enter the sales into the budget worksheet. Next, estimate your expenses by month referring to your Action Plans to ensure you have accounted for all of the expenses necessary to implement your plan. Fine tune sales and/or expenses until you are satisfied with the results.

## One Page Performance Scorecards

The disciplined tracking of your results and progress is critical for achieving the Objectives in your One Page Business Plan. We encourage you to create a Scorecard for each of your Objectives and update them monthly.

## Even More Sample Plans

Included are an additional fifteen One Page Business Plans that can be accessed with Microsoft Word®.

## ... and 10 Bonus Tools

Your CD Toolkit contains 10 very practical and powerful bonus tools not included in the book. Be sure to explore your CD!

**Interactive Exercises, Forms and Templates**

**Sales Calculators**

**One Page Budget Worksheet**

**Performance Scorecards**

**Extra Sample Plans**

# Contents

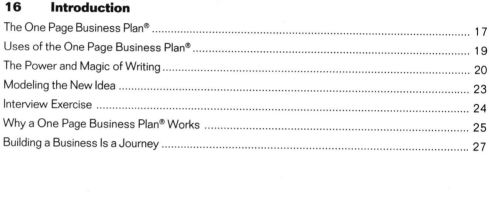

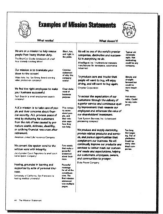

## 58    The Strategies

## 70    The Plans

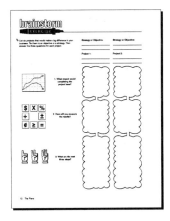

## 78    You Did It!

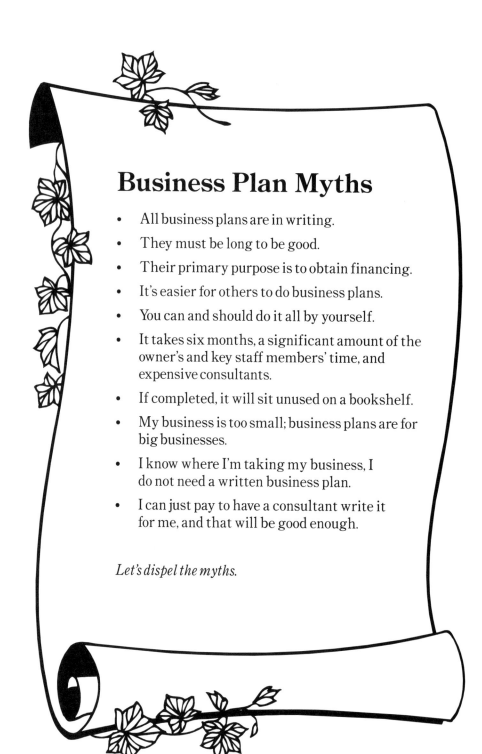

# Business Plan Myths

- All business plans are in writing.

- They must be long to be good.

- Their primary purpose is to obtain financing.

- It's easier for others to do business plans.

- You can and should do it all by yourself.

- It takes six months, a significant amount of the owner's and key staff members' time, and expensive consultants.

- If completed, it will sit unused on a bookshelf.

- My business is too small; business plans are for big businesses.

- I know where I'm taking my business, I do not need a written business plan.

- I can just pay to have a consultant write it for me, and that will be good enough.

*Let's dispel the myths.*

# Introduction

## The One Page Business Plan®

*Visionaries are the keepers of the dreams.*

*Entrepreneurs take risks and make the dreams real.*

*The community nurtures and supports creative businesses.*

Every business owner has a business plan. Meet a business owner at a party and most likely you will hear the majority of that plan within 30 minutes. Of course they will boast about their latest product success, and moan about employees, customers, and partner problems. If you listen, you'll also hear them freely describe their vision, objectives, strategies, and their plans.

Business plans don't have to be long to be good. A single page can contain all of the essential elements you need to tell your employees, board of directors, potential partners, or banker where you are taking your business and how you are going to get there. This book is going to show you how to do that.

The most important reason to have a business plan is to clarify your thinking, regardless of the size of your company. Is it possible to have too much clarity or focus? How much of your time and your business resources are wasted on projects that detract from your primary mission? What could you accomplish if everyone in your organization really knew what you were trying to do? To have a business plan is to be clear about where you are taking your business. When you're clear, and it's in writing, others will know and understand your vision and how you plan to get there.

Extensive business plans are required by those people and organizations who have money that you want. They have specific requirements that must be met or you will not get their money. This book is not about those business plans, but can greatly simplify their preparation. If you can get focused and clear on one page, you can then turn each short phrase into a paragraph, a full page, a chapter, etc. It is always easy to expand, it's much more difficult to focus and simplify. Mark Twain once said, "give me three weeks and I'll write you a short letter."

It doesn't have to take six months of agonizing meetings, pounds of written documents, endless spreadsheets, and complicated flowcharts to produce a meaningful business plan. It also does not take an army of expensive consultants. A few well-constructed phrases and short sentences can say a lot. The examples in this book will demonstrate that for you.

> *"The most important reason to have a business plan is to clarify your thinking, regardless of the size of your company."*

You and your team know your business, inside and out. You know your industry – the major trends. You talk with your competitors and suppliers regularly. You read the newspaper, and trade journals, and maybe even surf the net a little. You also share your dreams with your close friends, associates, and family. You have everything you need to draft the plan in your head. You could draft it this morning and have a meaningful discussion with someone you trust this afternoon. If you want to bring in a consultant to help, great! Give them a copy of your draft and interview them. If they have valuable insights, hire them and have them help you refine it.

Business planning concepts are not difficult. You already understand all of them. You dream about your business, you set goals, and you work throughout the year in an organized manner to make it all happen. You probably would like to do it with less stress and better results. That's why the concept of a one page plan sounds good to you.

Why must you have a written plan? You know where you are going. But without a written plan, it's always subject to change. Every time you talk about it, it will be different. Put it in writing and everyone sees the same thing.

If writing a business plan still seems too big of a task, even after reading this book, get another business owner to commit to doing his or her plan at the same time. It's kind of like going to the health club with a friend. Get a planning partner, commit to a process, and set some deadlines. Serve as coach and cheerleader to your planning partner. It works. I know because I got writer's block when I attempted to write my own. A fellow entrepreneur gently but firmly guided and challenged me through the process. I did the same for him.

A business plan brings out the best and worst in most business professionals. It facilitates creative and analytical thinking, problem solving, communications, interfunctional sharing, and teamwork. It generates hope and enthusiasm about the future. It also brings out procrastination, frustration, differences of opinions, and possibly anger. It is not a benign process. But when done well, the process is very valuable and has its own sense of satisfaction. Your business will be stronger.

**The One Page Business Plan**

- vision
- mission
- objectives
- strategies
- plans

# Uses of The One Page Business Plan®

There are many uses for the One Page Business Plan.® Listed below are four categories with many different uses. This list is obviously not exhaustive but meant to give you an idea of some of its uses to date. Keep blank copies of the One Page Business Plan® handy. If you find yourself dreaming about a new product, service, business, or career, start taking notes. Capture your thoughts as they come.

### External Presentation

- Complete business plan for small to mid-size companies
- Vehicle for testing business ideas with your board of directors, partners, banker, and employees
- Draft concept for Small Business Administration loan or venture capital funding business plan
- Summarizes existing plan

### Inspiration and Motivation

- Tool to get back on track if you've lost your vision
- Career planning

### Research and Development

- Place to summarize ideas for new division or new business
- Quick sketch and fleshing out of idea for new product or service
- Process for planning major projects

### Internal Process Guide

- Complete business plan for small to mid-size companies
- Business plan for subsidiaries or divisions of larger corporations
- Functional or departmental planning tool (sales, marketing, finance, etc.)
- Strategic planning starting point for CEOs in larger corporations
- Methodology to quickly update annual plan for significant mid-year changes
- Summarizes existing plan

"Writing takes time, usually much more time than talk. The written word requires a certain level of artfulness and thoughtfulness in expression. In writing, we do not ramble on and on, as we do in speech. We choose our words more carefully. The words remain to be reread, refined, a source for reflection and mindful change if necessary."

— Thomas Moore
*Care of the Soul and Soulmates*

# The Power and Magic of Writing

*"Writing allows others to participate in your dream and give you feedback."*

There is magic in the written word! Especially when they're your words about an idea that you have been thinking and talking about for sometime. Somehow the process of writing initiates the transformation from idea to reality. It also does many other wonderful things.

Things get clearer when you write. Of course at first the process can feel very awkward, and the results seem poor and anything but clear. But given time and patience, the process results in a connection of the mind with the reality of the paper. Thoughts begin to develop into images. Images turn into key words and short phrases. An outline begins to emerge, and the clarity builds.

If you stick with your writing, you also get focused. In the beginning, you'll have many ideas, more than you can ever implement. But the process of capturing them on paper results in a conscious and unconscious ranking and prioritization. I believe it is important to capture as many of your thoughts regarding your product, service, or business as possible without critiquing them. The natural process of writing will keep the best and strongest of your ideas. Your vision and mission will become more concise through this evolutionary process, resulting in a focused approach.

Writing allows others to participate in your dream and give you feedback. Writing provides a consistent forum, whereas in conversation the context changes each time you speak. Allowing others to participate and help support your idea to its next step is crucial to your overall success. The lone ranger mentality is no longer necessary nor effective.

The written word also produces a contract with yourself that results in immediate action. Haven't you found that if you make up a grocery list and leave it at home you almost always remember everything on the list? Many users of The One Page Business Plan® report that as soon as they begin to write their action items – some of which they have been thinking about for years – they start to take action on them. *I think it's magic!*

1. Architects visualize the details of a new building and produce a simple sketch to see how it might look.

2. Songwriters mentally hear a new melody and then test it out on a piano to see how it will sound.

3. Movie producers imagine the setting of their next picture and produce storyboards to help them produce a more complete image of their story.

# Modeling the New Idea

> *"...business owners need a way to test their ideas without having to put their cash or business at high risk."*

Architects, songwriters, movie producers, and inventors make models in some shape or form so they can see their ideas in a more visual, concrete manner. This process is one of the early steps that makes an idea something real and tangible. Models are a technique to help with the visualization of ideas.

As creators of businesses, we need a methodology for exploring our business ideas. It's too difficult, expensive, and nonproductive to produce working models or samples for every potential idea that comes our way. Market research is also very expensive and is generally reserved for our very best ideas. Complicated products with long lead times, requiring expensive raw materials and manufacturing facilities, obviously cannot be produced and tested like a new melody on the piano. And yet business owners need a way to test their ideas without having to put their cash or business at high risk.

Most individuals in business check out their ideas in conversation with trusted associates, consultants, friends, and relatives. But conversation is fluid, flexible, and frequently informal. Also we may not deliver the same message and details to everyone; hence the response we receive may be affected by the way we presented our thoughts. A melody played from written music will sound similar regardless of the piano it's played on. Unfortunately the spoken word is subject to much greater ambiguity when delivered.

Business people do however have the written word to describe their thoughts and ideas. The written word allows the sharing of our ideas with others in a consistent, clear fashion. The business plan is, in effect, our modeling tool. It provides the sketch, the vision, the road map for our ideas. In many ways, it's just like the composer's first few chords; the musician gets to hear it and so do others. The business plan works the same way. You get to see your ideas in writing and so do others.

# INTERVIEW
### e x e r c i s e

↳ Ask your planning partner or a fellow business owner to interview you with the questions below. Tape the session so both of you can take notes from the recorder afterwards. Then write each person's notes below. ⧖ 30 minutes

Describe your business. Where are you going with it? What will it look like in five years?

What market need will your company's product or service fulfill? Why are you in this business? What's your passion?

What would you like to celebrate this year? What would you like to celebrate this time, next year?

What has made your business successful to date? What will make your business successful over time?

What business-building projects are on your to-do list? What have you been procrastinating on that you know would make a difference in your business?

# Why The One Page Business Plan® Works

*Business plans don't have to be complex and cumbersome. The One Page Business Plan® is meant to be simple and to help you get focused quickly.*

### Simplicity

The One Page Business Plan® is effective because it takes a complex subject and makes it simple. It's easy to read and understand. If you are the writer, you will know when you are finished because you have effectively covered all of the important elements of your business plan.

### Focus

The One Page Business Plan® works because it focuses on what's important. There is no room for fluff or filler. The use of key words and short phrases tells your reader that only the essence is being presented for review. The fact that this business plan is only one page communicates that the investment in reading is limited.

### Readily Understandable

The five elements of the One Page Business Plan® are readily understandable. As you read each section, the business plan element telegraphs the kind of information being presented. You know the vision statement is going to be expansive and idealistic. You expect the mission statement to be powerful and customer oriented. Objectives should be realistic and measurable. Strategies are well thought out, and plans are action oriented.

### Versatility

The One Page Business Plan® works because it's a tool for communication. If you are the owner of a business, this one page document can be an important tool for communicating to your existing or prospective employees, partners, shareholders, investors, or banker the kind of company you are building and how you plan to build it.

### Consistency

It's an effective communication tool because you send the same message to every person you give it to – unlike the spoken word, which may change every time you speak. Additionally, with the written word, you have chosen your words carefully and you are communicating only the most important elements of your business plan.

### Flexibility

The One Page Business Plan® works because it's easy to change and update with your latest thinking. An important thought in the morning can be in your plan that afternoon. Capturing those "moments of clarity" quickly and in a useful manner will preserve them for further review, consideration, and possible action.

So what's the benefit of having a one page plan? It's your plan, your ideas, in your words. It's a reference point for any significant business or financial decision you may be considering. It's simple, concise, and it's you. Bankers, investors, and potential partners can have a complete overview of your business at a glance. Attach your budget and you're ready for a meaningful discussion about your business.

# Building a Business Is a Journey...

*The business plan is your map!*

> *"Had you considered that Queen Isabella of Spain was one of the most powerful and important venture capitalists of all time?"*

Building a business is a journey, it always has been. Marco Polo, Christopher Columbus, and Ferdinand Magellan were all great adventurers who took extended journeys. These journeys were explorations into the unknown parts of the world seeking new lands, exotic spices, fame, and fortune. These explorers were also businessmen and many of them had venture capitalists. Had you considered that Queen Isabella of Spain was one of the most powerful and important venture capitalists of all time?

Great journeys start with a vision. The vision is the dream. It describes what the journey is about and what you hope to find or create. Columbus's vision was to reach the Indies by sailing west.

All great journeys also have a mission. The mission describes the purpose for the trip. Columbus wanted to prove the world was round. Queen Isabella's mission was different. She wanted the riches and the power that conquering the new lands would bring.

Journeys have specific goals or objectives that drive certain behavior. John F. Kennedy wanted to have a man on the moon by the end of the 1960s. This goal focused many people's energy into specific actions to achieve this deadline. That's the purpose of a well-defined objective; it produces meaningful action.

Strategies set the direction. They are the road signs. They help to keep you on target so that you ultimately achieve your destination. Great strategies remain constant over the entire journey; Columbus kept heading west and it worked! Establish clear strategies for building and growing your business and stick to them.

Successful journeys have a plan. The plan details the important actions that must be taken to make the venture a success.

Wherever you are, today is the starting point. Develop a business plan that guides the building of your business. Use your business plan as a map to keep you on track to your destination.

# A Vision Statement That Works:

To build Phoenix Electronic Controls, Inc. into the premier industrial process control company in the Southwest.

Within five years grow PEC, Inc. to $20 million in revenues by expanding its role from a manufacturing representative business to a value-added company offering complete engineering, field service, and integration engineering services.

# The Vision Statement

## What are you building?

*"The Vision Statement should describe your idea in a manner that captures the passion of the idea."*

The vision section of The One Page Business Plan® is very important. It's the place where you get to describe your vision, your way! Vision statements should be expansive and idealistic. They should stimulate thinking, communicate passion, and paint a very graphic picture of the business you want. Great vision statements are fun to read. When written well, they can trigger emotional and sensory reactions. If perchance you are looking for investors, a great vision statement is essential.

There is another important reason to create a large vision. When you describe your vision in an expanded manner, you are inviting others to help you see possibilities you might not see. I believe vision statements are all about exploration, creating possibilities, and asking "what if" and "why not."

You can hardly exaggerate your vision statement. Go ahead and write a wildly optimistic, no limits, maybe even outrageous, vision statement. Ask your friends and associates to push you to think "way out of the box." Then live with what you wrote for a while. Don't rush into the editing process. It may just turn out that you decide to build something more exciting than you originally believed possible.

Don't sanitize your vision statement. Keep it full of passion. This is your opportunity to describe your dream. This section of the business plan is not the place to be analytical. If you describe a limited vision, one that is dull and boring, how can you expect to be excited about your business? And if you aren't excited, how can you expect to be successful? If you don't capture the passion you feel, others will have difficulty getting interested in your project. In fact, investors typically say that the dream is almost always worth more than the reality.

The key to capturing your vision is to be free flowing and not to restrict the flow of any thoughts. Capture all thoughts that come to your mind and use powerful adjectives to describe all the characteristics. Be sure to include the personal elements of your vision, as this is the source of your passion that will carry you through the difficult and frustrating times.

Your vision has evolved over time and will continue to change. Don't allow future ideas to impede your writing today. Describe your vision as you see it now!

# Your Vision...

👉 As you think about the questions on these two pages, write down any words or short phrases that come to mind in the "idea balloons" below.

## WHAT?

Products or services? or both? How many?

Company Image: What will this company be known for?

Owner's Role: What is your role? How will you spend your time?

editing
research
writing coach

6 jobs per
month
minimum

all star concepts

## WHERE?

Business: Local, regional, national or international?

Customers: Where are they? What cities, states, countries?

Business Operations: Headquarters, sales offices, manufacturing, etc.?

## WHO?

Customers: Who are they? (most businesses have several types of customers)

Strategic Alliances: Who can you partner with?

Advisors: Who can provide professional and strategic advice and help you grow this business properly?

# Creating the Company You Want

Don't worry about answering all of the questions; just try to capture your immediate thoughts.

### WHEN?

Start-up: When will this business be operational?

Facilities: When will office/manufacturing/distribution space be required?

Systems: When must they be selected, tested, and operational?

### WHY?

Owner: Why am I creating this business?

Customers: Why will they buy these products or services?

Investors/Bankers: Why will they invest/loan money to this business?

### HOW?

Financing: How will this business be financed?

Culture: How do you want to interact with employees, suppliers, customers?

Personal Beliefs: How will your personal beliefs about business impact this business?

# INTERVIEW
### e x e r c i s e

This exercise helps you envision the kind of company you want (and don't want) in terms of products and services, customers, and the work environment. Sometimes, it's easier to answer the questions on the right first. Have your planning partner lead you through this exercise.

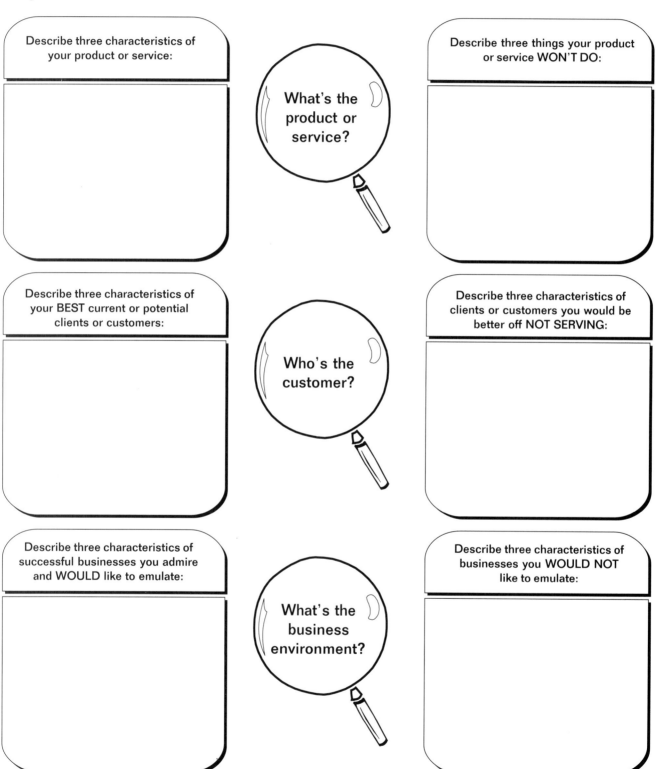

**Describe three characteristics of your product or service:**

**What's the product or service?**

**Describe three things your product or service WON'T DO:**

**Describe three characteristics of your BEST current or potential clients or customers:**

**Who's the customer?**

**Describe three characteristics of clients or customers you would be better off NOT SERVING:**

**Describe three characteristics of successful businesses you admire and WOULD like to emulate:**

**What's the business environment?**

**Describe three characteristics of businesses you WOULD NOT like to emulate:**

# Crafting Your Vision Statement

👉 STEP 1: Create a vision statement by filling in the blanks below. Have another person read it back to you.

**Vision Statement (first draft)**

Within the next _____ **years, grow** _____ **into**
company name

**a $** _____ ☐ local ☐ regional ☐ national ☐ international _____
annual sales                                                                type or description of business

**providing** _____
description of products and/or services

**to** _____
describe your customers

STEP 2: Rewrite the vision statement above, modifying it using your own words:

_____

_____

_____

_____

_____

STEP 3: Now write a wildly optimistic, no limits, outrageous vision statement!

# Examples of Vision Statements .........

Vision statements are individualized and stylistic. Here are 11 statements written by small to mid-sized business owners, with comments about what works well for each:

**Sounds intriguing and innovative. Playful and yet stimulating. It's a large vision but very believable.**

Create a network of Creativity Cafes around the world that are live and cyberspace networking salons featuring educational entertainment and electronic cyber theater. A fun place where people gather for play and work; where creative people, using the marriage of art and technology learn from each other and have a forum for showcasing their work.

Creativity Cafe™

**Narrative style. Personal, yet professional.**

McAniff Consulting envisions a business that does excellent consulting work with small to medium clients in the Northwest and large companies nationally. The consulting work will emphasize the integration of the three "P"s of Planning, Process, and Performance to achieve excellent business results. My vision is to share office space and interact with other management consulting professionals to develop a successful practice.

McAniff Consulting

**Reflects owners' personal style and commitment to change and values. Business concept well defined.**

To create an innovative global consulting and training firm to support the emergence of a new paradigm in business using the Core Group Process as its foundation.

Guiding Principles:

• Experience joy! Create a satisfying and fulfilling experience for all of us.

• Model processes that are the foundation of this business.

PeopleAssets (Innovative Consulting and Training Services for Tomorrow's Business)

**Offers a lot of information about the company. Includes elements of mission statement. States what is important to owners.**

GeoCentral is a Napa-based company that is known globally for its:

• Commitment to sharing earth's finest treasures by offering innovative products that showcase the richness and diversity of nature.

• Educating and promoting people's connection to this planet.

• Customer orientation, quality products, personal service, and retail earnings opportunity.

Locally, GeoCentral is known for its beautiful, open, artistic offices, motivated employees, and community contributions.

GeoCentral

| | |
|---|---|
| Very clear description of business. Appeals with humor. | To produce a weekly, wacky fun food show for national syndication where we take the everyday job of cooking and dish out some super easy, low-fat recipes and top it off with ladles of laughs. We want to become known as the Joan Rivers of cooking.<br>The ShortCut Cooks... |
| Personal with important statement of key elements. | California Knits is a creative, soul-filled enterprise that provides:<br>• vibrant, unique, comfortable clothing as art for women.<br>• custom design capabilities for individual clients.<br>• training and mentoring of the next generation of machine knit artists.<br>California Knits |
| Concise. Important statements regarding location, products, and customers. | Build a successful local business furniture company that specializes in providing competitively priced furniture with superior service to companies with 10 to 50 employees.<br>Custom Business Interiors |
| Clear description of business. Product described very elegantly, yet friendly and inviting to use. | To manufacture and distribute nationally, incredibly delicious crepes, ready to serve instantly, for any occasion, from the most elegant to the most informal.<br>Crepes dianne |
| Concise. Solid definition of business. | In Northern California, become the premiere full home service company and the leading industrial and municipal sewer/pipeline maintenance company.<br>Sanact Inc. (dba Roto Rooter) |
| Concise, clear, and powerful! | To have Design Media become recognized as the world leader in web-based training and educational delivery systems.<br>Design Media |
| Short and powerful. Makes you want to know more. | To become recognized as the world leader in toys and games that entertain and educate.<br>DaMert Company |

. . . . . . . . . . . . . . . . . . . . . . . . . . . . **That Work!**

# FEEDBACK
### e x e r c i s e

🖐 Take a few days to reflect on the three vision statements you wrote on page 33. Then share them with a couple of friends or associates. Use this page to take notes and incorporate their feedback into your vision statement.
⌛ 60 minutes, 30 minutes per person.

First Person Feedback

Second Person Feedback

_____

_____

_____

_____

_____

_____

_____

_____

Note here key words and phrases from above or other sources you would like to use in your own vision statement:

# summarize

✍ Rewrite your vision statement below. Use your own style to describe your vision and choose words that are comfortable and meaningful to you.

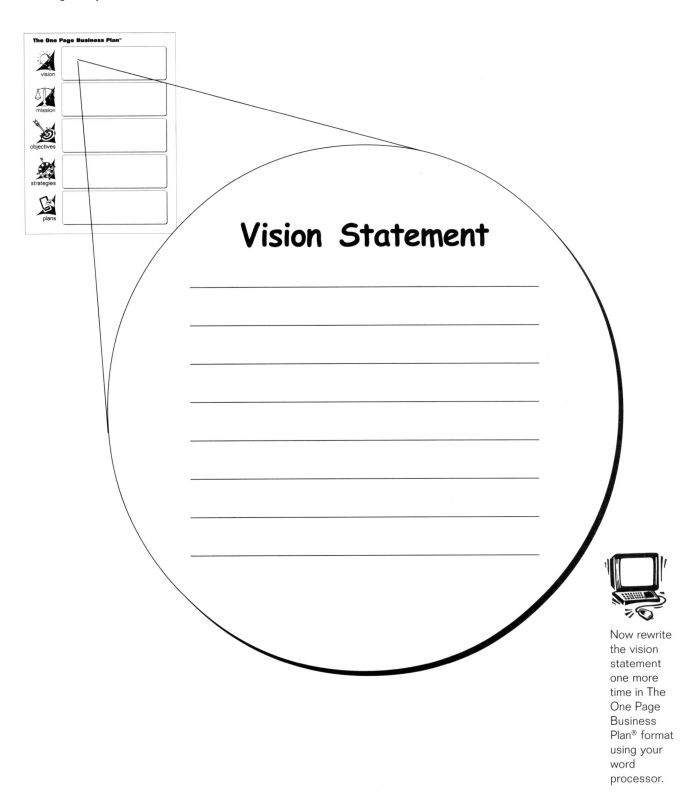

**The One Page Business Plan™**

vision

mission

objectives

strategies

plans

## Vision Statement

_____

_____

_____

_____

_____

_____

_____

Now rewrite the vision statement one more time in The One Page Business Plan® format using your word processor.

# A Mission Statement That Works:

DaMert Company's mission is to create FUTURE CLASSIC products that capture...the wonders of the world around us, the magic of our imagination, the spark of innovation within each of us, and the mysteries of the future.

DaMert Company
(an international toy and gift company)

# The Mission Statement

## Why does this business exist?

*Mission Statements always answer the question, "Why will customers buy this product or service?"*

The mission statement describes the purpose for which your product, service, or business exists. Great mission statements are short and memorable. They communicate in just a few words the company's focus and what is being provided to customers. They always answer the question, "Why will customers buy this product or service?"

There is a current trend towards making mission statements very clear and focused. Often just a few words can truly describe a company's essence. For example, — Nike's *Just Do It*, Tandem Computer's *Total Reliability, No Limits*, or FEDEX's *The World On Time* are powerful statements about their mission. While these examples are more typically considered tag lines or company slogans, they communicate volumes about these companies in just a few words. That's what a good mission statement should do. Your initial mission statement is likely to be multiple sentences, but try to keep it concise and powerful.

Mission statements are also about commitments and promises. Ask yourself, "What is your company committed to providing your customers or constituencies?" Under what circumstances would you refund your customer's money and apologize for not providing what was promised? What would you be willing to do to make amends with a dissatisfied customer?

The answers to these questions may help you to understand why your business exists. Consider them carefully.

Successful businesses balance meeting the needs of their customers with meeting their own needs. This balance is delicate, but it must be addressed in order for your business to succeed. Failure to define both your customer's and your needs may make the business equation out of balance. "Out of balance" can ultimately translate to "out of business" or being in a business that you don't like, want, or understand.

Mission statements are not about money. Include your financial goals in your vision statement and quantify them in the objectives, but leave them out of the mission statement. Pursuing an idea primarily to satisfy the need for money usually results in an unsatisfying business.

Mission statements must reflect the owner's passion and commitment. When the business satisfies an owner's passion for creativity, independence, or the need to serve others, there is substance and staying power in the mission. With a clear mission, you'll have the grounding necessary to see you through the tough times. If you're not well grounded, you may abandon your company when the seas get too rough.

# Your Mission...

Use these questions to reflect on why your business will be successful. Capture your thoughts using key words and short phrases.

**1** What is the product or service? What differentiates you from the competition?

**2** Describe your ideal customers.

# What's in it for the customer and you?

**3** Why will customers buy this product or service? What value does this product or service provide the customer? What unique benefits does this product or service provide the customer?

**4** What passion(s) are you trying to satisfy by building this business? What beliefs do you have about business that will impact this business? What is the highest good that this business can achieve? What values will drive this business? Who will benefit from this business?

# INTERVIEW
## exercise

↪ The interviewer writes down your answers to the questions on the left. As you ask the interviewer to restate what he/she heard you say, write your notes on the right. ⧖ 30 minutes

| The Interviewer | You |
| --- | --- |
| Why will customers buy your company's product or service? | Answer restated: |
| What is your company committed to providing your customers? | Answer restated: |
| What can your company promise? | Answer restated: |
| What passion(s) are you trying to satisfy by building this business? | Answer restated: |

# Crafting Your
# Mission Statement

Federal Express exists solely for one reason: Overnight Package Delivery.

## Exercise

Experiment with 1 – 6 key words that describe why your company exists from your customer's point of view. Capture your competitive marketing edge or unique selling proposition.

1st Attempt _____

2nd Attempt _____

*Does this mission support your vision?*

# Examples of Mission Statements

## What works! | What doesn't!

We are on a mission to help rescue people from heavy kitchen duty.

The ShortCut Cooks (producers of a half hour comedy cooking show)

*Short, fun, and right to the point.*

Our mission is to translate your ideas to the screen!

Video Arts, Inc. (an Emmy Award-winning video production company)

*Concise statement of why this company exists!*

We find the right employees to make your business successful.

Tech Search (a small employment search company)

*Clear statement of business purpose.*

AUL's mission is to take care of people and their concerns about financial security. AUL provides peace of mind by sheltering its customers from the risk of loss caused by premature death, sickness, disability, or outliving financial resources after retirement.

American United Life Insurance Company

*This company cares about people, and their mission says how they can help.*

We convert the spoken word to the written word with integrity.

Jack London Court Reporters (a small court transcription company)

*Few words that make a powerful statement about business.*

Healing, grounded in learning and supported by acts of personal kindness.

University of California, San Francisco (a leading medical university)

*Powerful message for all of the constituencies. The first mission statement was multiple pages.*

We will be one of the world's premier companies, distinctive and successful in everything we do.

AlliedSignal, Inc. (multinational materials manufacturer for aerospace, automotive industries)

*Typical old corporate style. Not motivating, could be any company.*

To produce cars and trucks that people will want to buy, will enjoy driving, and will want to buy again.

Chrysler Corporation

*Simple and straightforward but could be more inspiring.*

To exceed the expectation of our customers through the delivery of superior service and continuous quality improvement that rewards our employees and enhances the value of our shareholders' investment.

Total System Services, Inc. (a bankcard processing company)

*Not memorable. Could be any company.*

We produce and supply electricity, provide related products and services, and pursue opportunities that complement our business. We will continually improve our products and services to better meet our customers' needs and expectations, helping our customers, employees, owners, and communities to prosper.

Duke Power Company

*Too long. Not inspiring. Full of platitudes. Could be many electrical companies.*

# Other Mission Statements ...........................

**Personally made the way you want it.**

A specialty, custom craft company

**The purpose of the Bay Area Entrepreneur Association is to provide: education, networking, and support for new, prospective, and experienced entrepreneurs in the San Francisco Bay Area.**

Bay Area Entrepreneur Association

**We help you get out of bed feeling great so that you can experience the day the way you want to.**

East West Healing Arts Center

**We do for families what no one should ever have to do.**

Crime Site Cleanup Company

**Total Reliability. No limits.**

Tandem Computers

**We move at the speed of business.**

United Parcel Service

**It's about communications between people... the rest is technology.**

Ericsson (a global telecommunications company)

**To provide color, light, and energizing beauty in comfortable, natural fiber clothing.**

California Knits

**To provide growing companies a single source for purchasing all of their office furniture from an experienced professional that understands how to create attractive, functional, flexible, and affordable office layouts.**

Custom Business Interiors

**Help us lose weight. Recycle bimonthly.**

Sacramento Waste Management

**We bring the taste of India to your home.**

Bhurji Indian Grocery Store

**Bring light, air and the beauty of nature into homes through creative windows!**

Colorado Garden Window Company

**Establish the Creativity Cafe as the *New School for the Next Millennium.* To inspire and empower the public in both cyberspace and in communities around the world by providing affordable access to technology and instruction and by creating experiences that inspire and educate us to be better human beings.**

Creativity Cafe™

**Helping people see better, one hour at a time.**

LensCrafters

..................................... **That Work!**

# FEEDBACK
e x e r c i s e

Review your mission statements on page 43 and the examples on pages 44 and 45. Is yours too long? Unclear? Refine your mission statement below and then discuss it with two people. Use their feedback to complete your final version.
⏳ 60 minutes, 30 minutes per person.

Use the examples on the preceding pages to help you refine your mission statement:

First Person Feedback

Second Person Feedback

Rewrite your mission statement below. Experiment with different adjectives and verbs. It may help to move on to another section and come back to summarize your mission statement.

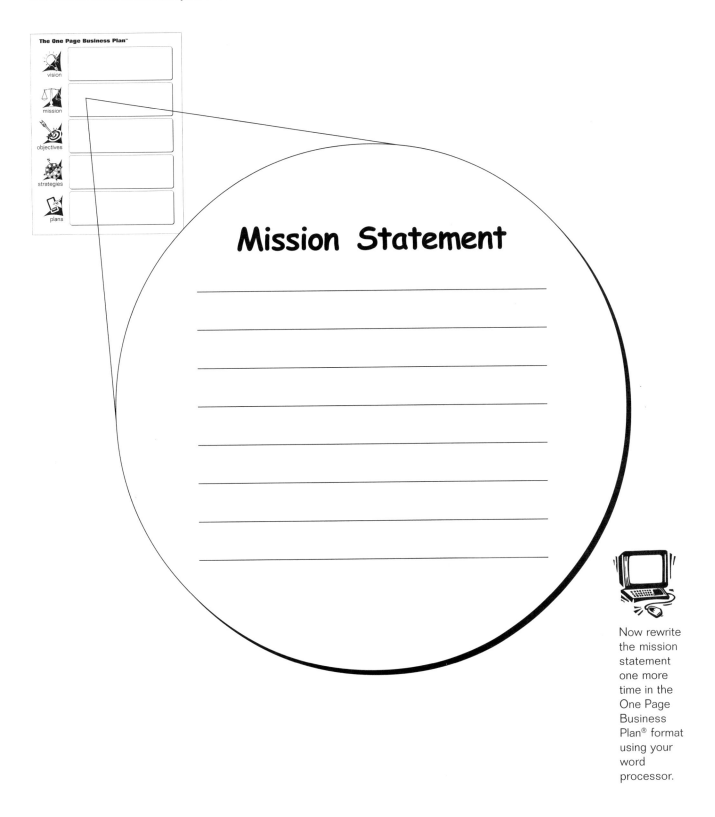

**Mission Statement**

Now rewrite the mission statement one more time in the One Page Business Plan® format using your word processor.

# Objectives That Work:

2003 Objectives for Sports Apparel Company…

Grow sales to $5.5m in 2003, $7.0m in 2004, and $9.0m in 2005.

Achieve profit before tax of $480,000 in 2003, increase to 10% of sales by 2005.

Introduce approximately 15 new products in 2003, achieving sales of $750,000.

Increase number of existing accounts with greater than $100m volume from 8 in 2002 to 15 in 2003.

Secure two major product license agreements: NBA and NFL by 6/30/03 yielding $500,000 each.

Reduce shipping expense to 3% of sales, starting in 1st quarter.

Aggressively manage inventory to budgeted levels, maintain active inventory at 93%.

Reduce overtime to 3% of total manufacturing hours.

# The Objectives

## What results will you measure?

Objectives clarify what it is you are trying to accomplish in specific, measurable goals. For an objective to be effective, it needs to be a well-defined target with quantifiable elements that are measurable.

Zig Ziglar, a nationally known motivational speaker, says in order to achieve the goals that are important, you must become a *meaningful specific.* Meaningful specifics are those individuals who know what they want to achieve in very specific terms and have targets and time frames written down to help them get there. People who have vague ideas, with no target dates, never get to the finish line. Zig refers to these people as *wandering generalities.*

> "Meaningful specifics *are those individuals who know what they want to achieve in very specific terms and have targets and time frames written down to help them get there.*"

Whereas your vision statement is expansive and idealistic, and the mission statement short, powerful, memorable, and customer oriented, your objectives are designed to focus your resources on achieving specific results. The purpose of a well-defined objective is to cause meaningful action.

There are many types of objectives and your plan should include a wide variety. For many businesses the two most important categories will be the financial and marketing objectives. It is important, however, to tailor your objectives to cover the entire scope of your business, focusing on the goals that are most critical to your success.

Although there is no magical or precise number of objectives, The One Page Business Plan® can accommodate eight to nine different ones. If you have an objective for revenue, profitability, two or three for marketing, that leaves four or five to cover manufacturing, operations, personnel, and other important goals that are critical to your success.

Keep your objectives meaningful by making them specific and important. One of the most powerful aspects of the One Page Business Plan® is the limited amount of space. This requires prioritization and pruning to get to a list of only the most important goals.

The exercises in this section are designed to help you analyze the important objectives for your business to achieve. The exercises will focus you on past successes and failures, as these are a great source of ideas for creating goals. The examples are designed to demonstrate how to construct powerful goals.

Create objectives that can be measured and then measure the results throughout the year. Objectives are a prime tool for accountability. Stay focused and stay on track!

# What accomplishments would you like to celebrate...

Brainstorm three business accomplishments you would like to be celebrating at the end of this year and next year.

## ...this year?

## ...next year?

Imagine what you might say at the company celebration dinner:

**CONGRATULATIONS!**

"We successfully completed (____)."

"We are proud to announce the beginning of (____)."

"We no longer have to deal with (____) because we (____)."

"We increased (____) by (____)."

"We decreased (____) by (____)."

# brainstorm
## EXERCISE

# Where does success come from? What will it look like?

Think about your past experiences, what you have learned from these, and answer the questions on the left. Imagine what your future success will look like and respond to the questions on the right.

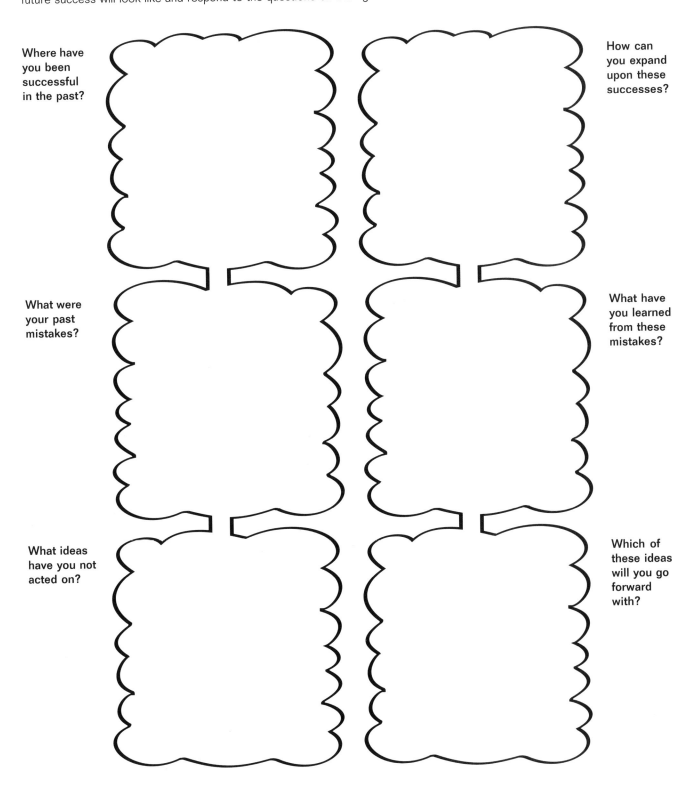

**Where have you been successful in the past?**

**How can you expand upon these successes?**

**What were your past mistakes?**

**What have you learned from these mistakes?**

**What ideas have you not acted on?**

**Which of these ideas will you go forward with?**

# What targets will you aim for?

🖖 Check at least six objectives below that are critical for your success. Check as many in each category as you find to be appropriate and add your own if necessary.

### Financial

- ☐ sales
- ☐ profit
- ☐ gross margin
- ☐ cash flow
- ☐ inventory
- ☐ owner compensation
- ☐ debt
- ☐ _____

### Marketing and Sales

- ☐ revenue
- ☐ units sold
- ☐ # of accounts
- ☐ # of new customers
- ☐ # of repeat customers
- ☐ advertising response rates
- ☐ sales per employee
- ☐ closing rate
- ☐ _____

### Operations

- ☐ job count
- ☐ units processed per hour
- ☐ service time
- ☐ shipping time
- ☐ error rates
- ☐ equipment downtime
- ☐ _____

### Human Resources

- ☐ compensation
- ☐ benefits
- ☐ safety
- ☐ morale
- ☐ environment
- ☐ overtime
- ☐ use of contractors
- ☐ training hours
- ☐ _____

## Examples of Objectives

**Financial**

- Increase sales to $1 million in 2003, $1.5 million in 2004.
- Increase product margin to 42%.
- Reduce cost of goods sold to 28% by purchasing in bulk containers.
- Reduce number of days in receivables from 48 to 35 by 6/30/03.
- Reduce interest expense by 20% by re-negotiating long-term notes.

**Marketing and Sales**

- Introduce 4 new products in 2nd qtr; 6 in 3rd qtr; 2003 incremental sales $500,000.
- Launch new account incentive program in 3rd qtr; goal 50 new accounts generating $20k per month.
- Improve sales per employee to $120k per quarter by May 31st.
- Obtain one major new account per quarter generating $150,000 per year.

**Operations**

- Achieve billable time of 75%.
- Reduce order entry errors to 24 per 10,000 orders.
- Ship 98% of orders same day and 100% of orders within 3 days.
- Produce and ship all special orders within 5 working days.
- Consolidate from 5 warehouses to 2 by 6/30/03; achieve annual savings of $500,000.
- Reduce customer service labor costs per order by 5% by 3/31/03.

**Human Resources**

- Reduce overtime to 8% or less by 3/31.
- Reduce turnover to 3%; implement job rotation program 1/1/03.
- Increase training hours per employee to 25 in 2003.
- Increase scholarship program participation to 300 students.

Use the examples of objectives below to help you decide which types of objectives are most important.

## R & D

- ☐ # of projects completed
- ☐ # of successful tests
- ☐ documentation rates
- ☐ safety incidents
- ☐ environmental emissions
- ☐ design productivity
- ☐ cost reduction
- ☐ _____

## Manufacturing

- ☐ production units/cost
- ☐ capacity
- ☐ quality
- ☐ dual sourcing %
- ☐ scrap rates
- ☐ labor efficiency
- ☐ downtime
- ☐ inventory levels
- ☐ _____

## Personal

- ☐ # of vacation days taken
- ☐ # of hours worked per week
- ☐ take home pay
- ☐ retirement
- ☐ education
- ☐ personal growth
- ☐ charitable contributions
- ☐ public speaking
- ☐ _____

## Other

- ☐ professional awards
- ☐ investors return
- ☐ banker covenents
- ☐ supplier reliablity
- ☐ government headaches
- ☐ community activities
- ☐ _____
- ☐ _____

## Examples of Objectives

- Complete 22 projects by June 30th
- Develop 14 prototypes for marketing samples by 1/15/03.
- Complete exploratory work on project *top cat* in 180 man-days.
- Decrease microbiology sample test costs to $1.50 per sample by 8/15..
- Automate laboratory documentation; reduce hours to 1.5 hours per page.

- Produce 1.3 million units in 2003.
- Expand packaging line to 2 million unit capacity by 12/31/03.
- Reduce production labor to 8% of sales by 12/31/03.
- Develop dual sources for household and hair care products; reduce COGS to 34% by 8/15.
- Cut loss time accidents to less than one per quarter.
- Improve manufacturing yield to 98%; achieve savings of $450,000.

- Commit to working no more than 50 hours per week; play on most weekends.
- Increase vacation to 3 weeks.
- Read one book per month.
- Exercise at least twice a week.
- Lose 20 pounds by yr end; 5 pounds per quarter.
- Mediate 20 minutes per day

- Conduct 4 pro-bono workshops per year at our church.
- Donate 100 hours of volunteer time per quarter.
- Commit to writing 5 pages per week on book.

# What does this business need to accomplish?

☝ Review the objective ideas you checked on the previous two pages. Choose four of them and answer the questions for each.

| **Describe the activity required:** | **What will happen and when?** | **What is the financial impact?** |
|---|---|---|
| **①** Type of objective: | | |
| | | |
| **②** Type of objective: | | |
| | | |
| **③** Type of objective: | | |
| | | |
| **④** Type of objective: | | |
| | | |

**EXAMPLE** Type of objective:   R&D

| Develop/introduce new products | A book 6/30; A tape 7/31 | Sales of $10,000 in 3rd qtr; $20,000 in 4th qtr |
|---|---|---|

# Crafting Meaningful Objectives

✍ Now rewrite the objectives on the left into sentences or phrases combining your responses in the four columns. The first two objectives will always be sales revenue and profitability.

**sales revenue objective:**

**profitability objective:**

**❶**

**❷**

**❸**

**❹**

## Will meeting these objectives accomplish your vision and mission?

**example:**

Introduce a book by 6/30 and an audio tape by 7/31, resulting in 2004 sales of $30,000.

# Examples of Objectives

## What works! | What doesn't!

| What works! | | What doesn't! | |
|---|---|---|---|
| Increase sales 25% to $4 million in 2003; $5 million in 2004, & $6.3 million in 2005. | Specific, measurable. | Develop a sustainable business; minimize peaks and valleys. | Not specific. No way to measure. |
| Obtain "Oracle Named Account Status" by July 2003; SunMicro key acct status by year end. Add $2.5 million in new sales. | Measurable, easily understood, accountability assigned! | Develop strategic marketing alliances with key partners. | Not specific. Which partners and when to achieve what? |
| Introduce new hair care line, 1st quarter, estimated 2003 sales of $250,000; skin care line 3rd quarter, estimated 2003 sales of $100,000. | Measurable, specific, financial impact known. | Develop and introduce new products to grow business. | Vague. Needs type of products, how many, and financial impact. |
| Improve overall product margin to 40% by reducing discounts on low volume accounts to 3%; enforce minimum new product margin target of 45%. | States goal and how it will be achieved. | Improve profitability and cash flow to support business growth. | Needs to be quantified. |
| Reduce overtime to maximum of 3%; introduce 401k by June 30th; implement recognition program by Sept. 30th. | Says how morale issue is going to be tackled and when. | Improve employee morale. | No way to measure. No statement of work to be done. |
| Reduce inventory to $950,000 by 9/30/03; maintain raw materials @ 1.5 months; finished goods @ 2 months. | Clear, measurable goals. | Reduce inventory levels. | Doesn't state the desired result. Might cause other problems. |

**summarize**

👉 Read your vision and mission statements again and rewrite your objectives below. Ask yourself again if these objectives will accomplish your vision and mission statements.

## Objectives

_____

_____

_____

_____

_____

_____

_____

_____

_____

_____

**The One Page Business Plan™**

vision

mission

objectives

strategies

plans

Now write your objectives once more in The One Page Business Plan® format using your word processor.

# Strategies for the 21st Century...

### Price isn't everything

Lots of customers will pay extra for a helpful, well-trained staff. Ask Nordstrom.

### Attract the very best employees and give them a stake in the business

Give rank-and-file employees a vested interest in how a company performs. Intel does.

### Think fast

Particularly in the high-tech world, move and evolve quickly. Learn from Netscape.

### Superior Execution

A well-executed plan for a simple product will beat a poor implementation of a great product everyday.

### Be visible, be a resource

Write articles, newsletters, books, web pages. Speak to any group that will hear you. Volunteer your time and expertise whenever you can.

### Don't try to do it all

Specialize in what you do best. Contract or forget the rest.

# The Strategies

## How will you grow this business?

Strategies set the direction, philosophy, values, and methodology for building and managing your company. Strategies also establish guidelines and boundaries for evaluating important business decisions. Following a predefined set of strategies is critical to keeping a business on track.

One way of understanding strategies is to think of them as "industry practices." Every industry has its leaders, its followers, and its rebels, and each has an approach for capturing market share. Pay attention to the successful businesses in your industry and you can learn important lessons. Miss an important lesson and your business may not even get off the ground.

Strategies are not secret. In fact they are common knowledge and openly shared in every industry. Pick up any industry's publication and you will know precisely what the industry's leaders have to say about the opportunities and how to capitalize on them. These leaders will also share their current problems and their solutions. This is critical information for building and managing your business.

In most industries there are four to six core strategies that the successful businesses follow. These core strategies are easy to understand, remain relatively constant over time, are used by market leaders, and result in growth and profitability.

*"Following a predefined set of strategies is critical to keeping a business on track."*

Great strategy statements can be broad and yet create tremendous focus. When you have the right strategies for your business, they will probably last for several years with minor changes. A significant breakthrough in your industry, or a significant change in your business, can of course cause you to revisit your strategies.

A properly constructed set of strategies will define your business and keep it focused. For example, a CPA whose vision is to build a local practice would be significantly off track to accept international clients who would take him out of the country on extended trips. An upscale boutique targeting high-income clientele would not be wise to locate right next door to a K-Mart. A labor-intensive product with low margins should probably not be made in New York City.

Strategies must address both internal and external influences that are affecting or may affect your business. External strategies capitalize on opportunities to grow the company or overcome outside threats. Internal strategies address issues related to the business's strengths and weaknesses in the areas of culture, capabilities, efficiency, and profitability.

Strategies provide the answer to the question: "What will make this business successful over time?"

# Key Elements to Building Your Business

✏ Check the boxes that represent those topics *critical* to growing and operating your business. Refer to your objectives while making your selections. Feel free to add to the list.

| | | | |
|---|---|---|---|
| ☐ Market Presence | ☐ Product Uniqueness | ☐ Company Image | ☐ Location |
| ☐ Employees | ☐ Technical Knowledge | ☐ Reputation | ☐ Visibility |
| ☐ Distribution Channel | ☐ Trademarks/Patents | ☐ Key Customers | ☐ Number of Accounts |
| ☐ Referrals | ☐ Customer Service | ☐ Quality | ☐ Technology/Equipment |
| ☐ Partners | ☐ Board of Advisors | ☐ Other People's Skills | ☐ Family Support/Money |
| ☐ Shared Support Services | ☐ Time Management | ☐ Capital | ☐ Strategic Alliances |
| ☐ Product Cost | ☐ Cash Flow | ☐ Trade Industry Acceptance | |

☐ _____

☐ _____

# Decide Which Strategies Are Appropriate for Your Business

Finding appropriate strategies for your business is not difficult. Much information is readily available to you for free or at minimal cost. Selecting strategies you can utilize is also not difficult.

Where do you find strategies specific to your business? Trade journals, local business newspapers, and national business magazines are great places to start. These publications are filled with current articles on industry trends in the critical areas of market-ing, finance, and operations. They are usually short, concise, and written by industry experts. They describe the problems and opportunities with which the industry is struggling and the solutions that businesses are implementing. A review of the contents for the last few issues will certainly give you a solid perspective on what's important in your industry and how the leading edge companies are planning their futures.

If you are starting a business, you'll have access to some important information that you will want to seriously consider before proceeding. Also, if this is a new business, and it requires funding, you can be sure the lender will want to know how you are planning to address these issues.

Other people that know your business can be very helpful in identifying and selecting strategies. Your banker, CPA, attorney, vendors, and employees have a lot of insight into your business. Ask them for their thoughts.

# RESEARCH
## exercise

Review the last three issues of your industry's trade association journal and answer the questions below.

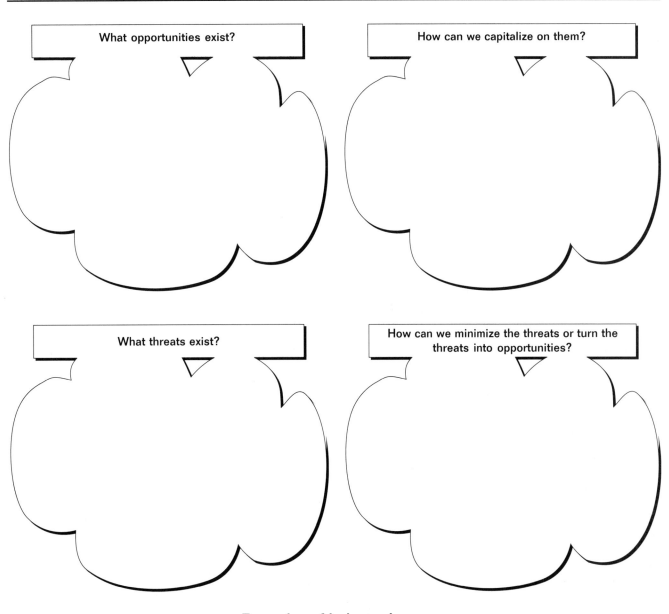

**What opportunities exist?**

**How can we capitalize on them?**

**What threats exist?**

**How can we minimize the threats or turn the threats into opportunities?**

## Examples of Industry Issues

| | | | |
|---|---|---|---|
| pricing | environment | economic | the public |
| customers | market | technology | taxes |
| suppliers | competition | media | import/export regulations |
| cost reduction | government | | |

# focus EXERCISE

# Who are your customers?

List and describe up to three categories of your **BEST CUSTOMERS**.

Use the words below to help brainstorm your customer descriptions:

age
sex
income
occupation
education
language
family size
countries
regions
size of cities
social class
lifestyle
personality
purchase frequency
purpose of purchase
brand loyalty
habits
hobbies

Use the following words to help brainstorm how you will promote and sell to your customers:

workshops
associations
newspapers
direct mail
outplacement agencies
referrals
partnerships
Internet
local retailers
television
radio
telemarketing
magazines
speaking
government agencies
trade journals

**❶**

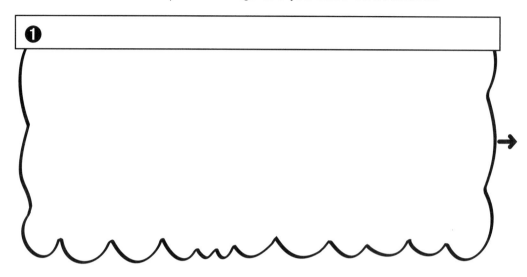

**❷**

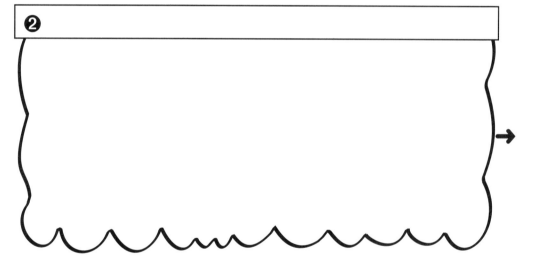

**❸**

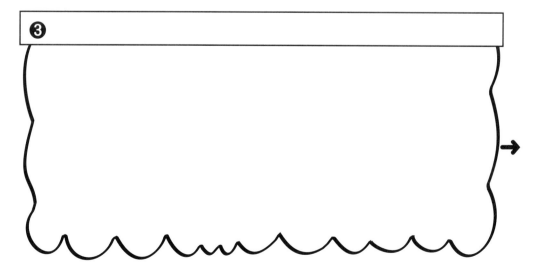

# How will you promote and sell to them?

Where/how do these customers buy your products now?
Where/how will they buy them in the future?

How do you plan to **PROMOTE** your products or services to these three categories of customers?

# What's working in your company?

It's just as important to know what works in your company as what doesn't. Use the keywords list at the bottom to help you brainstorm if you get stuck. (For established companies only.)

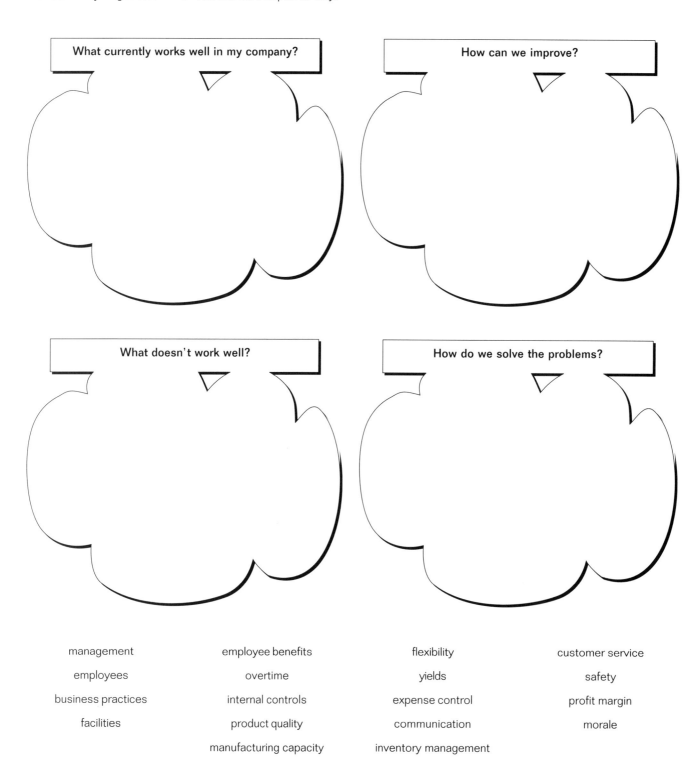

**What currently works well in my company?**

**How can we improve?**

**What doesn't work well?**

**How do we solve the problems?**

| | | | |
|---|---|---|---|
| management | employee benefits | flexibility | customer service |
| employees | overtime | yields | safety |
| business practices | internal controls | expense control | profit margin |
| facilities | product quality | communication | morale |
| | manufacturing capacity | inventory management | |

# Critical Issues Examination

focus EXERCISE

Select three critical issues that are limiting your company's growth, profitability, or effectiveness. This exercise helps you differentiate between symptoms and root causes so that you can see more clearly what needs to happen to achieve a permanent and effective change. (For established businesses only.)

| List 3 issues or symptoms: | What is the root cause of this? | What needs to change? | How will results be measured? |
|---|---|---|---|
| | | | |
| | | | |
| | | | |
| **EXAMPLE** Back orders are excessive! | No sales forecast, and capacity is too low | Develop monthly sales forecast by product and expand packaging | Track output per week vs. planned output; monitor back orders daily |

# How do we get from here to there?

☞ What has made your company successful or limited its growth to date? How will you build on the successes and overcome the current limitations to achieve your vision?

|  | **Current Business*** | **Vision** |
|---|---|---|
| **Success Factors** | | |
| **Limiting Factors** | | |

*Current business could be your business or industry

# Crafting Meaningful Strategies

☞ From the focus exercise on the previous page, select up to five areas that are critical to building your company. Draft a strategy statement for each one below.

**❶**

**❷**

**❸**

**❹**

**❺**

Do these strategies describe:    How the business will be built and managed?

How we will capitalize on market opportunities?

How we will solve our business's critical problems?

# Examples of Strategies

| What works! | | What doesn't! | |
|---|---|---|---|
| Position company for strategic acquisition in 2004; build brands, identity, management team, and profits. | Sets the direction with the big picture and exit strategy. | Make money, limit investment in business and employees, think about retirement at age 65. | Everything is wrong with this strategy. |
| Sell total solutions, not time, not parts. | Selling value, not time. Allows for much higher margins. | Employees: hire at the lowest possible wages, perform important functions ourselves. | Great employees are worth their weight in gold. |
| Employees: hire the best, have them just before we need them, retain them thru job satisfaction and equity participation. | Always need good people. Have a people strategy. | Ideal client: anyone who will buy our products and services. | It's impossible to be everything to everyone. Specialize. |
| Control expenses and growth; self-capitalize/bank finance company; achieve sales and profit plans. | Build a strong company with good internal controls. | Product: whatever is hot this year, we will sell. | Followers rarely have the volume or margin the leaders do. Invest in R&D. |
| Focus on web-based training and communications products with delivery via Internet, Intranet, CD Rom. | Defined set of products. Clear and understandable. | Increase prices to maintain margins. | Might work in the short run. Competitors will find a way to do it better for less. |
| Aim high with minimum project size of $300,000. | Sets lower limits. | Project size: all projects. | Not all clients or projects are profitable. Refer low-margin projects to your competitors. |

➷ Use this summary to refine your strategies by writing them below. Check each strategy for the following characteristics: easy to understand, constant over time, used by market leaders, and results in growth and profitability.

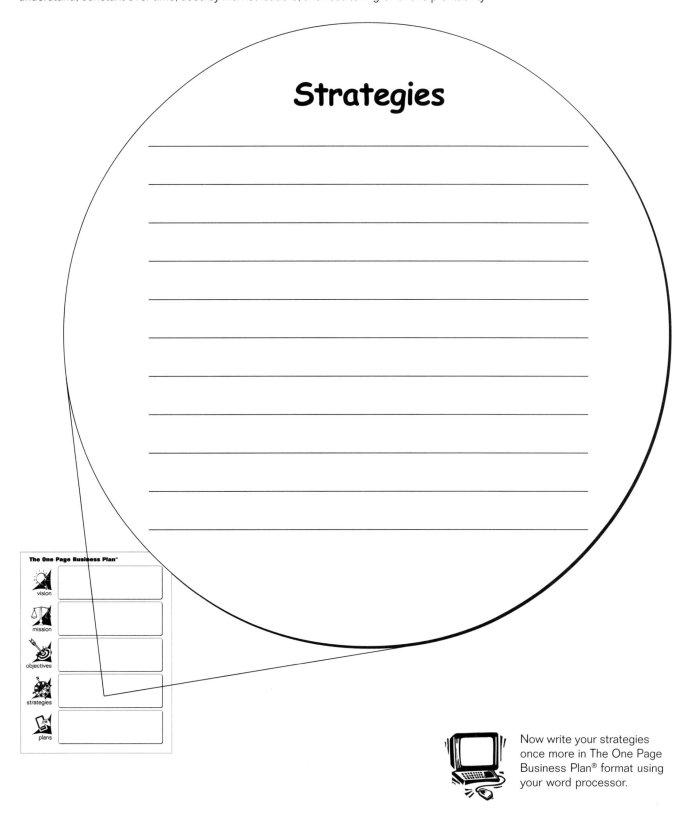

# Strategies

Now write your strategies once more in The One Page Business Plan® format using your word processor.

Strategies, objectives, and plans interrelate with each other:

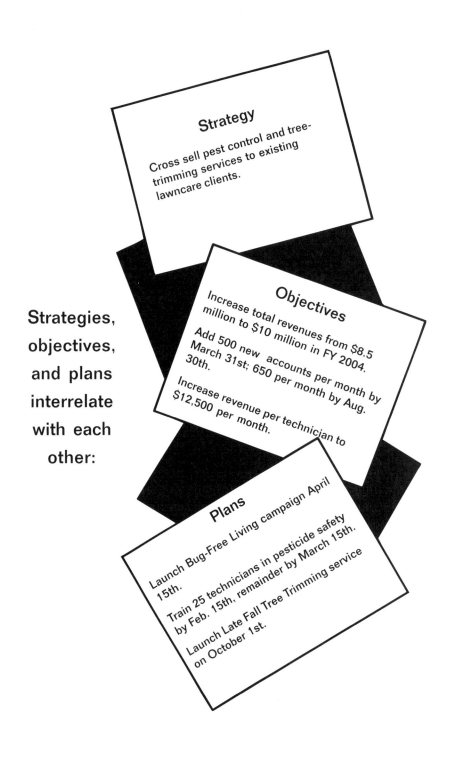

**Strategy**

Cross sell pest control and tree-trimming services to existing lawncare clients.

**Objectives**

Increase total revenues from $8.5 million to $10 million in FY 2004.

Add 500 new accounts per month by March 31st; 650 per month by Aug. 30th.

Increase revenue per technician to $12,500 per month.

**Plans**

Launch Bug-Free Living campaign April 15th.

Train 25 technicians in pesticide safety by Feb. 15th, remainder by March 15th.

Launch Late Fall Tree Trimming service on October 1st.

**The GreenLawn Company**

# The Plans

## What is the work to be done?

Plans are the specific actions the business must implement to achieve the objectives. Plan or action items should be important, significant, and contribute to the growth of your business. Each plan or action item is, in effect, a project.

Ideally, each plan statement should directly relate to an objective and a strategy. Plans should be action oriented, should specify specific tasks, and should have deadlines. If your business has employees, independent contractors, or utilizes outside resources to complete tasks, the ideal plan statement will identify who is responsible for performing each function.

Most business owners or prospective business owners have a to-do list a mile long. They struggle not with what needs to be done, but how to get it all done. The One Page Business Plan® is designed to keep you and your business focused on the important, but not necessarily urgent, business tasks. Steven Covey in *First Things First* writes about how easy it is to focus on the most important tasks every day and never get to the things that will really grow your business. By having your business-building action list clearly defined, and delegated appropriately, it becomes possible to complete those tasks that will build your business.

The exercises in this section are designed to guide you in the development and prioritization of your action plans and in relating them to specific objectives and or strategies. The exercises suggest that you prepare estimates of the financial or operational impact of each of these projects and determine in advance how you will measure the results. This process provides both an objective framework for selecting the projects with the highest benefit or payback and a method for postauditing the results.

In preparing your plans, estimate the cost and time frame for each project. Transfer this information into your budget worksheets, calculate the impact of your to-do list on your cash flow. I've learned that if you don't know what your projects will cost, it's quite likely you will not have enough cash to fund them. A project with no cash is like a car with no gas – it's not going very far.

Make your plans carefully. Execute them on time, within budget, and with excellence. Measure their impact routinely.

# brainstorm
## EXERCISE

List six projects that would make a big difference in your business. Tie them to an objective or a strategy. Then answer the three questions for each project.

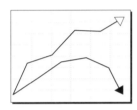

1. **What impact would completing the project have?**

2. **How will you measure the results?**

3. **What are the next three steps?**

**Strategy or Objective:**

_____

_____

**Project 1:**

_____

_____

**Strategy or Objective:**

_____

_____

**Project 2:**

_____

_____

# Business-Building Projects

Strategy or Objective:

_____

_____

Project 3:

_____

_____

Strategy or Objective:

_____

_____

Project 4:

_____

_____

Strategy or Objective:

_____

_____

Project 5:

_____

_____

Strategy or Objective:

_____

_____

Project 6:

_____

_____

# Integrating Objectives, Strategies, and Plans

✍ Choose five projects from the preceding two pages and complete the chart below.

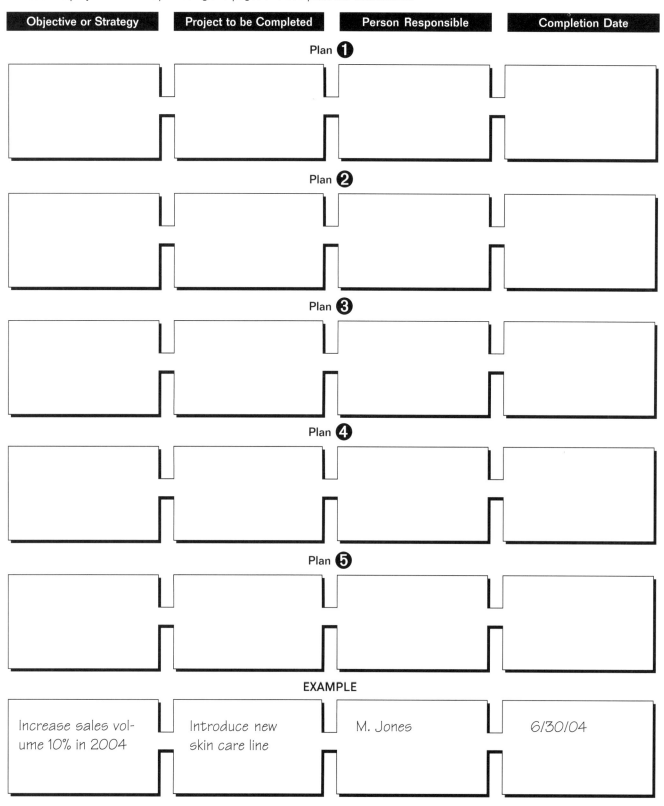

| Objective or Strategy | Project to be Completed | Person Responsible | Completion Date |
|---|---|---|---|
| **Plan ❶** | | | |
| | | | |
| **Plan ❷** | | | |
| | | | |
| **Plan ❸** | | | |
| | | | |
| **Plan ❹** | | | |
| | | | |
| **Plan ❺** | | | |
| | | | |
| **EXAMPLE** | | | |
| Increase sales volume 10% in 2004 | Introduce new skin care line | M. Jones | 6/30/04 |

# Crafting Meaningful Plans

Now rewrite the plans on the left into sentences or phrases, combining your responses in the four columns.

**①**

**②**

**③**

**④**

**⑤**

**●** example:

Complete new skin care line and have ready for Sept. '04 convention;
M. Jones project team leader

# Examples of Plans

| What works! | | What doesn't! | |
|---|---|---|---|
| Attend NY trade show in June; LA in September; and Chicago in October. | Identifies specific activity with dates. | Write annual employee reviews for R. Smith and B. Jones by 2/28. | Important activity but not a task that builds the business. |
| Complete phase III network design by 7/31. Utilize Berkeley Software, Inc. for QA review. | States work to be completed with completion date; identifies vendor. | Complete February financials by 3/15. | Routine activity; this is not a strategic business activity. |
| Overhaul skin care emulsion equipment during June shutdown. | Concise statement of time frame. | Implement new business practices. | Not specific; no dates and no accountability. |
| Hire route salesman for Sacramento territory in fourth quarter. | Specific position; some leeway for completion. | Hire approximately six new employees. | All new hires should be identified by position and approximate hire dates. |
| R. Smith to complete grant for handicap access upgrade by February 28. | Clear accountability and responsibility. | Develop committees for fund-raising. | When? Who is responsible? |
| Redo tax seminar marketing brochures in 2nd quarter. Bob Jones to lead team. | Specific with accountability. | Increase all prices during this year. | Not specific; should identify specific products. Percent increase should agree with budget assumptions. |
| Move to new Pleasanton facility October 15th. | Simple statement; allows others to plan accordingly. | | |

summarize

Use this summary to refine your plans by writing them below.

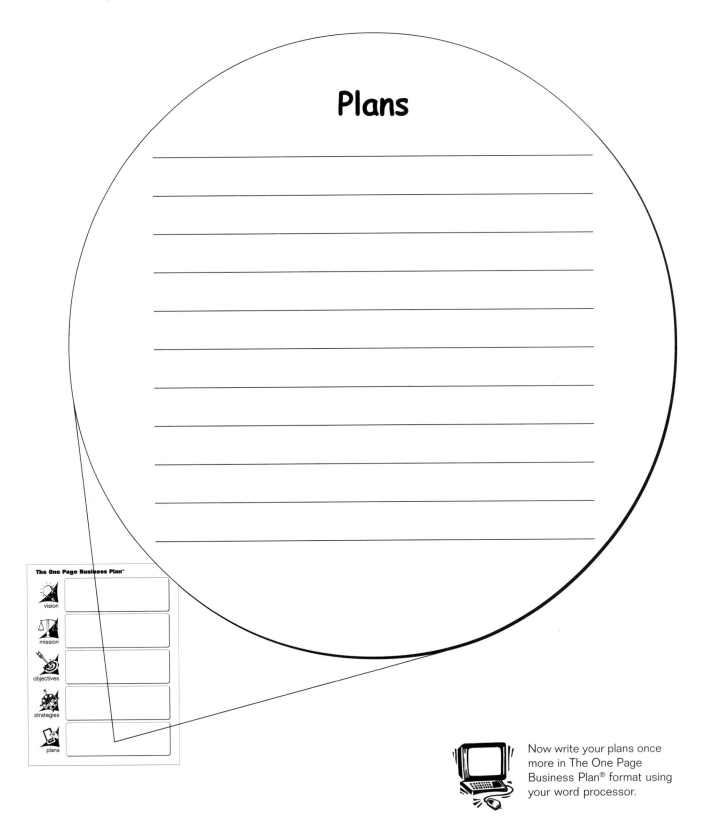

Plans

The One Page Business Plan™

vision

mission

objectives

strategies

plans

Now write your plans once more in The One Page Business Plan® format using your word processor.

*"He who chooses the beginning of a road chooses the place it leads to. It is the means that determine the end."*

— Harry Emerson Fosdick

You Did It! Congratulations! Your plan is now in writing. You are feeling a major sense of accomplishment. Go ahead and celebrate. This was hard work. Having your plan, in your words, on one page is a powerful business tool.

At this time you should have a final draft of your One Page Business Plan® in your word processor. Step back and review it. How does it look to you? If you are like most people, parts of your plan feel very tight and others still need some work. That's normal and OK. As you have learned by now, this process is iterative. Use the checklist on the following page to help make any minor editing changes that are necessary and you are ready to start sharing the complete plan. This is polishing; do not do a major rewrite at this time.

Now that you have your plan in a final draft form, it's time to put it to work.

You clarified and organized your thoughts into a concise business plan. Now others can respond to your plan.

# Polishing Checklist

### Overall Review

- Do the key words and short phrases describe the essence of your plan?
- Does your vision feel big, expansive, and exciting?
- Is your mission statement powerful?
- Are your objectives specific and measurable?
- Do your strategies state how you are going to build and manage this business over time?
- Are your plans action oriented and will they accomplish this year's objectives?

### Order and Abbreviation
(*Edit objectives, strategies, and plan statements to one line*)

- Eliminate all unnecessary words and phrases.
- Abbreviate words when necessary.
- Use symbols like "&" in lieu of "and" to save space.
- Use "k" or "m" for thousands, "M" for millions.
- Communicate the importance and priority of objectives, strategies, and plans by placing the most important ones first in each section.

### Creative Considerations
(*especially with layout of vision and mission statements*)

- Split sentences into multi-lines.
- Center text.
- Use bullets to make key points stand out.
- Double space to accent.
- Highlight key phrases in italics.

### Strengthening Exercises

- Draft and edit vision, mission and strategy until they are enduring statements that resonate with you, your partners, your management team, and key employees.
- Refine objectives and plan statements until they are very specific, measurable, and define clear accountability.
- Drop low-priority items; remember "less can produce more."
- Ask others for their comments.

# Putting the Plan into Action

Putting the plan into action is the most important step because the actions deliver the results you wanted when you started this process. For most entrepreneurs, this is easy. You are action oriented and can't wait to get started. Now is the time to put the plan to work. A few guidelines or suggestions for uses of the plan are summarized below:

### Use it to talk with your banker about financing.
Most bankers who have reviewed The One Page Business Plan® have found it to be an excellent tool for understanding both the business and the plans. It won't always lead to a loan being approved, and does not complete all the steps of the loan process, but it is an excellent start. Sharing your plan with your banker will get you useful feedback and lead to improved banker relations.

### Discuss your plan with investors.
Your completed One Page Business Plan® is an excellent tool for focusing discussions with present or potential investors. The plan shows what you intend to do and how you will make it happen. Combined with your enthusiasm and commitment, the plan will be a significant aid in getting investors and keeping them happy.

### Convert the plan into budgets.
Putting the plan into action usually requires quantifying the plans and objectives and getting the resources into place to support implementation. This is the process of budgeting. For many of my clients, this means going through the process of First Time Budgeting. Don't be afraid of it! Budgets help define the resources we need and provide the measures that allow us to know we are on track. If you need help in budgeting, get it. This is an important part of your path to success.

### Manage the implementation.
Planning is a vital first step toward success but not the last step. Implementing the plan and making it work is the vital next step. More companies fail because of *Failure To Implement* than for any other reason. Managing the implementation is the process of using the goals, plans, measures, and other tools that we have defined and making sure that the actions take place and are in line with the defined strategies, objectives, and plans. Everyone must be held accountable for meeting their goals. Frequent reviews and continuous monitoring of results will help move you toward the defined goals. *Failure To Implement* is not acceptable and must be dealt with immediately.

**External Presentation**
- Complete business plan for small to mid-size companies
- Vehicle for testing business ideas with your board of directors, partners, banker, and employees
- Draft concept for Small Business Administration loan or venture capital funding business plan
- Summarizes existing plan

**Inspiration and Motivation**
- Tool to get back on track if you've lost your vision
- Career planning

**R&D**
- Place to summarize ideas for new division or new business
- Quick sketch and fleshing out of idea for new product or service
- Process for planning major projects

**Internal Process Guide**
- Complete business plan for small to mid-size companies
- Business plan for subsidiaries or divisions of larger corporations
- Functional or departmental planning tool (sales, marketing, finance, etc.)
- Strategic planning starting point for CEOs in larger corporations
- Methodology to quickly update annual plan for significant mid-year changes
- Summarizes existing plan

**Keep the plan
with you.**

**Update it with
new thoughts.**

**Share it
with people
you trust and whose
opinions you value.**

**Measure your
progress at least
quarterly.**

**Prepare a
budget to match
the plan.**

### Make a copy for everyone.

Have them post it on the wall of their office. Plans need to be communicated and understood to help drive the necessary decisions and actions that will lead to success. Certainly, all your managers and employees should have a copy of your plan. Others you may want to share it with could include your advisors, bankers, accountants, suppliers, key customers, and key community members. Share it with anyone who could help your business succeed. Remember that communities support entrepreneurs, but they must first know about you to support you.

### Review your plan at team and company meetings.

Get some energy going around it. Implementing the plan means paying attention to it. Don't let it sit on a shelf. Your One Page Business Plan® is a working document that will work for you if you continually use it to remind your team and your employees about where you are going and how you will get there.

### Use it as a decision-making tool.

Managers make decisions on the fly every day. The One Page Business Plan® is the guide they should use to make those decisions. Does the proposed action support where the company is going? How would we decide on this item based on the plan? The strategies, objectives, and plans are very clear guides on where resources should be used and what the priorities should be. The vision and mission are more general guides that help determine the overall direction and the values and principles that apply. The plan as a whole is the prime decision making document that should be checked when key business decision are made.

Useful plans drive decisions and actions and get everyone working toward the same goals. Decisions and actions that help implement the plan are positive and support the success of the company. Decisions and actions that go in different directions significantly reduce the probable success of the business. We plan in order to focus our actions and decisions to achieve the desired results. Words which sum up The One Page Business Plan® process are:

### Focus → Action → Results

The plan provides the focus, and then we implement through actions guided by the plan. The planned actions lead to the results. When in doubt at this point, act. Sometimes try several actions, monitor the results quickly and carefully, and then decide on the best course of action to continue.

# One Page Business Plan® Samples

As you modify your plan over time, use the following pages of sample plans to give you ideas for refining your content or design.

## PeopleAssets
### Innovative Consulting and Training Services for Tomorrow's Businesses

vision

Within the next 3 years, grow CGP into a $3 million national consulting firm specializing in creative leadership development programs for Fortune 1000 companies.

mission

We help companies develop effective leaders!

objectives

- Increase revenue to 1.8 million in FY 2004.
- Increase gross margin to 54% from 32% by 12/31/04
- Earn a pretax profit of $450,000 for FY 2004.
- By 12/31/04, establish a client base of at least 10 companies.

strategies

- Leverage CGPs worldwide identity as entree into business consulting.
- Build company awareness by networking at executive level.
- Create simple, easily-produced materials from existing CGP products.
- Use first clients to define product offering/build momentum.
- Use a train the trainer approach to maximize reach in larger clients.
- Create product ranges so that any business can afford a system.

plans

- Develop written marketing plan by 2/16/04.
- Trademark Core Group Process by 4/4/04.
- Publish 4 quarterly newsletters, send to the first 1500 prospects on 3/15.
- Deliver 5 workshops by 6/30, and another 4 in Q3.
- Create high quality company brochure by 7/1/04.
- Create four mini-books on personnel management techniques by 12/31.

# Z - TEC, Inc.

vision

Within the next three years build Z-TEC International into a $50 million enterprise software solutions company specializing in integrated work-flow management solutions for large industrial process firms.

mission

Streamline the flow of work...in large industrial production facilities!

objectives

- Grow 2004 Revenue 20% to at least $27 Million.
- Achieve 2004 Profit before Interest & Taxes of $3.5 Million.
- Complete at least 8 new installations; yield fees of $6 million.
- Obtain 16 new clients w/ average project size of $500,000.
- Reduce accounts receivables from 63 days to 40 days by April 30th
- Migrate at least 20 existing clients to web-product by Sept. 30th.
- Reduce employee turnover from 25% to less than 10% by Q4.

strategies

- Growth: 50% each yr by developing new clients & migration of existing clients.
- Reputation:Product leadership & reputation from existing client referrals.
- Partners:Align w/industry leaders, partner for mktg & new products.
- Competitive Position:Optimize user-based pricing & modular system for flexibility.
- Products:Configure more than customize, business rules vs. custom programs.
- R&D:Work-flow solutions, open systems, multiple environments, object oriented.
- Resources: have people & systems resources in place before they are needed.
- Aligned team, know the plan, sense of urgency, responsibility/accountability.
- Use Employee Incentives to share rewards, create excitement & have Fun.

plans

- Implement financial reporting system at project/dept level by May 31st.
- Establish Software Forum for sharing project mgt & tech. issues by June 30.
- Measure progress against the business plan and allow for quarterly updates.
- Develop Sales & Marketing Resource Plan by 3rd quarter 2004.
- Develop partner strategies w/ Oracle, Sun Micro, IBM. by Oct. 31st.
- Implement Professional Skills Programs in Nov.; Mgt Development in Dec.
- Complete sales showroom remodel by Aug. 15th.
- Implement contractor peakwork load program by Sept. 15th.
- Upgrade internal systems including server, network, workstations by Dec. 31.

**A high-tech company**

# All-Right Engineering, Inc.

**VISION:**

Develop economically viable solution to 6782 printer memory error problem.

**MISSION:**

Reduce the incidence of printer fatal error messages.

**OBJECTIVES:**

Achieve .0000032 per thousand memory errors per average test cycle by 9/1/04.
Keep cost of upgrade to $1.53 per shipped unit.
Operate within budget of $356,000.00

**STRATEGIES:**

Use 3 teams of 2 engineers plus 2 outside consultants.
Concentrate on fixing current design rather that replacing it with another.
Hold weekly progress meeting with team to review progress against plan/budget.
Use outside consultants on as needed basis for new laser technologies.

**PLANS:**

Establish teams by 3/1.
Identify and qualify 2 outside consultants by 3/1; finalize contracts by 3/1.
Complete problem assessment by 5/31.
Propose an engineering solution by 6/30
Complete prototypes by 7/31
Complete product trials by 8/30.
Document final product specs by 9/30.
Complete installation of modified production equipment by 11/30.

**A Research and Development Firm**

**Synergen Associates, Inc.**
Management Team Development Process

### Vision

Within the next 12 months, evolve the existing management team into a vital growing force that:
- Fuels the growth of the company by seeing and being a part of the larger vision.
- Builds on its own energy and successes; learns from its failures/shortfalls.
- Expands capacity to contribute to the overall management of the company.
- Develops an espirit de corps that is supportive of the individual, the team, and the company.
- Design work style/culture that is adaptable/flexible to move quickly to meet customers needs.

### Mission

Build a management team that builds the business.

### Objectives

- Improve quality of decision making (measurement to be determined).
- Decrease amount of time to achieve management buy-in on key projects (measurement TBD).
- Reduce average time in management meetings from 25 hours/month to 12.
- Reduce average work week for management from 60 hours to 45 hours.
- Increase internal promotion ratio from 5% to 25%.
- Decrease management turnover from 20% a year to 5%.

### Strategies

- Evolve the management team over time; do not go for immediate, but temporary fixes.
- Encourage growth/participation; do not push team faster than they can grow.
- Transfer skills from president to mgt. staff; provide training and coaching as required.
- Allow for small errors, learn from all mistakes, and celebrate the successes
- Minimize fanfare about the process; let team respond to positive, subtle changes.

### Plans

- Implement business planning and budgeting process starting on November 2nd.
- Design and implement financial reporting system at Level 2 by Jan. 31st.
- Implement monthly business review sessions starting 2/24.
- Utilize CGC Consulting Group to facilitate quarterly development meetings starting Mar. 15th.
- Implement new managers training program in June; New supervisors training in August.
- Complete development of new employee orientation web-based learning module by 9/30.

**Management Development**

**Bay Area Entrepreneur Association...**
the Association for Self-Employment Success!

**VISION**

Build BAEA into a nationally recognized micro-enterprise organization with an extensive greater San Francisco Bay Area network of entrepreneurial support groups providing nationally recognized products, programs and services to entrepreneurs, small-business owners and partner organizations.

**MISSION**

The mission of the Bay Area Entrepreneur Association is to positively impact the community by creating viable businesses and successful entrepreneurial leaders through networking, support and connection to resources.

**OBJECTIVES**

- Increase total revenues from $125,00 to $350,000 in FY2004
- Increase membership from 500 to 750 by December 31st.
- Launch 4 networks by June 30th; 6 additional networks by Dec. 31st.
- Generate $35,000 from entrepreneurial programs, events and products in FY 2004.
- Conduct 24 workshops/programs generate $18,000 in gross profit.
- Conduct 4 Corporate Connection programs with 400 attendees; generate $8,000 profit.
- Increase low-income/minority memberships from 50 to 100 by Sept. 30th.
- Award 10 scholarships totaling $10,000 in FY 2004.

**STRATEGIES**

- Use public relations and media to share successes, educate, recruit and fund BAEA.
- Market and sell BAEA endorsed products and services nationally.
- Collaborate with natl micro-enterprise org. in national awareness programs and funding.
- Establish BAEA center to create long-term community presence & financial asset base.
- Attract/retain low-income entrepreneurs by offering scholarships funded by corp. sponsors.
- Utilize multi-lingual/cultural programs to attract minority entrepreneurs.
- Package successful BAEA programs & products to sell to other micro-enterprise organizations.
- Use technology to manage growth, streamline operations, deliver programs, & sell products.

**PLANS**

- Complete funding plan by March 15th.
- Hire executive director by May 15th.
- Expand board of directors from 5 to 9 by August 31st.
- Develop BAEA product and service marketing plan by Sept. 15th.
- Develop 2-year network expansion plan by October 31st.
- Launch sales/marketing plan of One Page Business Plan by Nov. 15th.
- Collect /write 20 success stories by Aug. 1st. Implement public relations plan by Nov.1st.

**A non-profit association**

# California Knits

## 2004 Business Plan

### Vision

California Knits is a creative, soul-filled enterprise that provides:
- vibrant, unique, comfortable clothing as art for women.
- custom design capabilities for individual clients.
- training and mentoring of the next generation of machine knit artists.

### Mission

To provide color, light, and energizing beauty
in comfortable, natural fiber clothing,

### Objectives

- 2004 Revenue $150,000.
- Achieve profit margin of 50% by holding production labor to 18%.
- Increase active store count to 20, an increase of 30% over last year.
- Outsource 50% of production by 4th quarter; produce 3,000 garments
- Add three new designs; 2 ready-to-wear, 1 gallery collectible; 1st yr sales $30,000
- Attend at least six trade/trunk shows in 2004; yielding  sales of $40,000

### Strategies

- Produce gallery quality garments to attract high-end consumers, galleries, & collectors.
- Design products w/ multiple price points; attract attention w/ gallery quality garments, but have affordable products available at $150 - $200 price point.
- Build network & professional relationships w/in fashion & garment industry.
- Outsource ready-to-wear lines, reserve personal time to create one-of-a-kind garments.
- Develop professional team for production and operation of business.
- Cultivate relationships with upscale clients for referrals and shows.
- Explore avenues to entertainment industry for costume and personal clients.

### Plans

- Develop budget and plans for capital needs for business by 4/04.
- Complete 2 ready-to-wear designs for show in Aspen in April.
- Contact six (list attached) fashion magazines; present portfolio for publication.
- Submit 10 applications (list attached) for retail and wholesale craft fairs (2/04).
- Attend three trunk shows: New York, June; Santa Fe, August, Carmel, October.
- Continue to send garments to consignment galleries where advantageous.
- Complete redesign of display booths for fairs by March 15th.
- Hire interns or apprentices for in-house production, maintenance, office work (2/04).

**A specialty manufacturing company**

# Phoenix Electronic Controls, Inc. — Business Plan

**VISION**

> To build Phoenix Electronic Controls, Inc. into the premier
> industrial process control company in the Southwest by
> expanding its role from a manufacturing rep. company to
> a valued-added rep. company offering complete engineering,
> field service, and integration engineering services.

**MISSION**

> PEC's mission is to help its clients control their processes
> and
> to provide an effective marketing, sales, service,
> and distribution channel for its manufacturers.

**OBJECTIVES**

Grow business 20% & achieve total sales revenues of $8 million in 2004.

Establish presence in muni market; secure $500,000 Tucson muni contract in 2nd Qtr.

Land at least 8 system projects at a minimum of $100,000 each in 2004.

Increase gross margin from 14.8% to 15.5%.

Achieve net profit of $300,000, an increase of 50% over last year's $200,000.

Increase sales per employee from $500,000 to $600,000.

Reduce Accounts Receivables from 58 days to 40 days by June 30.

**STRATEGIES**

Sell total solutions, not parts.

Build value-added services capability: engineering, service, eng. integration services.

Expand market geographically into Nevada and Colorado.

Aggressively target muni market & large scale processing manufacturers.

Increase margins by selling bundled parts & service; make cust. support a profit center.

Increase outside sales force effectiveness by strengthening sales support function.

Control expenses & growth, self-capitalize/bank finance, achieve sales & profit plans.

Develop autonomous, self-directed & controlled management team.

Share growth & prosperity w/ employees through incentive & equity participation.

**PLANS**

Complete 2004 business plan & budgets - Jan. 04, commit to qtrly bus & fin. review.

Write business plan for Tucson muni contract - 1st Qtr.

Develop marketing program for major systems sales - 1st Qtr.

Organize & staff sales territories; reduce discounts from 5% to 4% - Jan. 04.

Hire Tech Support Mgr. & Service Group Mgr. in 1st Qtr.

Purchase Colorado company or develop plan to expand w/ internal resources - 1st Qtr.

Develop incentive comp. programs for sales support & key employees - 1st Qtr.

Host two user seminars for key clients: April & Sept.

**A distribution / manufacturing representative company**

# Custom Business Interiors
## 2004 Business Plan

### Vision

Build a successful business furniture company that specializies in providing competitively priced furniture with superior service to companies with 10 to 50 employees.

### Mission

To provide growing companies a single source for purchasing all of their office furniture and equipment from an experienced professional that understands how to create attractive, functionable, flexible, and affordable office layouts.

### Objectives

- Generate sales of $500,000 and profits of $100,000 in 2004.
- Increase gross margin from 28% to 35%.
- Increase # of orders at $10,000 level to 50% of business; $25,000 to 20%.
- Conduct 15 "workspace efficiency" workshops for small businesses.
- Limit personal work time to 40 hrs; will hire assistant in Feb.

### Strategies

- Build reputation for excellent service; become the Nordstrom of office furniture.
- Focus on growth companies in Contra Costa, Alameda, and Solano counties.
- Target market to financial institutions, insurance & computer companies.
- Keep competitive price advantage by keeping overhead low.
- Sell via catalogs and not invest in showrooms or inventory.

### Plans

- Complete revised marketing brochure & mail to existing clients  Jan. 31st.
- Complete research on two new suppliers by June 04; annouce in Aug.
- Add PC-based design and layout software in May; announce in Aug.
- Redesign ACT! database by April to simplify direct mail process.
- Notify network by Jan. 15th regarding hiring plans for assistant.

**A business-to-business product / service company**

# E Management Book

## VISION

Become nationally known author, publisher, and consultant
serving entreprenuers and independent business owners.

~

- Consult primarily in SF Bay Area; approximately 30% of my time.
- Create products (books, tapes, CD's) for the entrepreneurial market (25%).
- Speak extensively regionally, building to national recognition.

## MISSION

Simplify the business of business for entrepreneurs.

~

Create professional business tools,
for entrepreneurs that build strong businesses.

## OBJECTIVES

Complete E Management book by 6/27; print 500 cc's in July.
Publish article in Inc. Magazine 4th qtr 2004 or 1st qtr 2005.
Sell 1,000 books in 2004; 25m in 2005; 50m in 2005; 100m in 2007.
First Fortune 1000 client in 2004, four in 2005; yielding consulting revenues of $50k per client
One national convention speaking engagement in 2004, four in 2005.
Ten registered/certified E Mgt. practitioners by 12/31/04; 100 by 12/31/05.
Complete E Mgt. audio tape by 8/31/04; annual sales of $50,000
Complete Breakthrough Business book w/R. Miller by 12/31/04; annual sales of $35,000.

## STRATEGIES

Collaborate to complete; can't do this by myself...Always keep it simple!
Use network/personal contacts to create opports to speak, get reviews, articles published.
Self-publish to start, prove marketability, seek national publisher.
Continue to turn consulting processes into products; products into programs.
Create products & programs for others to sell that serve the entrepreneurial market.
Seek endorsements/approval/intros/quotes from noted authors, CEOs, SBA.
Build brand & corporate identity.
Exit strategy: sell to major publisher or business training company in 5 - 7 yrs.

## PLANS

Develop publicity & marketing plan by 7/31.
Develop E Management practitioners program by 7/31.
Contract w/ Audio Design Productions for audio tape production 4/04.
Submit articles to Inc, Entrepreneur, Home Base Business for Dec. publication.
Complete mailing to 250 trade associations by 10/03 for speaking engagements.
Schedule 4 meetings w/R. Miller to complete 2nd book; 9/15 & 30, 10/15 & 10/31.

**A business plan for a product**

# Would you like to share your One Page Business Plan® with others?

Show us how well this process worked for you by sending us a copy of your One Page Business Plan®. Please be sure to include your name, phone number and your responses to the survey on the following page.

**The One Page**  **Business Plan® Company**

1798 Fifth Street
Berkeley, CA 94710

Phone:
(510) 705-8400

Fax:
(510) 705-8403

jhoran@onepagebusinessplan.com
www.onepagebusinessplan.com

# We want your feedback!

We appreciate the opportunity to act upon your feedback. Please take a minute to answer the questions below and fax to **510-705-8403**.

## How easy was each section to understand and complete?
### 1 = very easy   5 = somewhat difficult

| 1 | 2 | 3 | 4 | 5 | |
|---|---|---|---|---|---|
| ❑ | ❑ | ❑ | ❑ | ❑ | The Vision Statement |
| ❑ | ❑ | ❑ | ❑ | ❑ | The Mission Statement |
| ❑ | ❑ | ❑ | ❑ | ❑ | The Objectives |
| ❑ | ❑ | ❑ | ❑ | ❑ | The Strategies |
| ❑ | ❑ | ❑ | ❑ | ❑ | The Plans |

## Who are you?

❑ Entrepreneur (with an existing business)

❑ Entrepreneur (starting your first business)

❑ Corporation or corporate division

❑ Nonprofit organization

❑ _____

## How long did it take to complete your One Page Business Plan®?

## How have you used or how do you plan to use your One Page Business Plan®?

## How did you hear about The One Page Business Plan® and where did you purchase it?

## What success have you experienced as a result of learning about or using The One Page Business Plan®?

Do you have any suggestions or other comments?

_____

_____

_____

**THANK YOU!**

If you would like to receive literature from The One Page Business Plan® Company, please complete the information below:

_____     _____
NAME                                                                    COMPANY NAME

_____     _____
ADDRESS                                                                CITY, STATE AND ZIP

_____     _____     _____
PHONE                                           FAX                                              E-MAIL

# The One Page  Business Plan® Company

**If you would like additional information
on products or services, please contact
The One Page Business Plan® Company:**

The One Page Business Plan® Company
1798 Fifth Street
Berkeley, CA 94710

Phone:
(510) 705-8400

Fax:
(510) 705-8403

jhoran@onepagebusinessplan.com
www.onepagebusinessplan.com

# CALL 1-800-852-4890 TO ORDER TODAY FOR ONLY $34.95

NAME

COMPANY NAME

ADDRESS

CITY, STATE AND ZIP

PHONE                    FAX                    E-MAIL

☐ Put me on your list to receive the latest updates on *One Page Business Plan*® products and services.

**Credit Card Payments Only**

Call **1-800-852-4890** or fax your order to **707-838-2220**

☐ VISA    ☐ MasterCard    ☐ American Express    ☐ Discover

| | | | | | | | | | | | | | | | | | | |

SIGNATURE                                    EXPIRATION DATE

FOR PAYMENTS BY CHECK, PLEASE MAIL TO RAYNE FULFILLMENT, P.O. BOX 726, WINDSOR, CA 95492

| # OF BOOKS | PRICE EACH | TOTAL |
|---|---|---|
| | $34.95 | |
| Add 8.0% sales tax for California deliveries | | |
| Add $4.50 S&H for the first book and $1.00 for each additional book | | |
| **Total amount due** | | |

---

# CALL 1-800-852-4890 TO ORDER TODAY FOR ONLY $34.95

NAME

COMPANY NAME

ADDRESS

CITY, STATE AND ZIP

PHONE                    FAX                    E-MAIL

☐ Put me on your list to receive the latest updates on *One Page Business Plan*® products and services.

**Credit Card Payments Only**

Call **1-800-852-4890** or fax your order to **707-838-2220**

☐ VISA    ☐ MasterCard    ☐ American Express    ☐ Discover

| | | | | | | | | | | | | | | | | | | |

SIGNATURE                                    EXPIRATION DATE

FOR PAYMENTS BY CHECK, PLEASE MAIL TO RAYNE FULFILLMENT, P.O. BOX 726, WINDSOR, CA 95492

| # OF BOOKS | PRICE EACH | TOTAL |
|---|---|---|
| | $34.95 | |
| Add 8.0% sales tax for California deliveries | | |
| Add $4.50 S&H for the first book and $1.00 for each additional book | | |
| **Total amount due** | | |

# The One Page  Business Plan® Company

**If you would like additional information on products or services, please contact The One Page Business Plan® Company:**

The One Page Business Plan® Company
1798 Fifth Street
Berkeley, CA 94710

Phone:
(510) 705-8400

Fax:
(510) 705-8403

jhoran@onepagebusinessplan.com
www.onepagebusinessplan.com

# The One Page  Business Plan® Company

---

## Workshops and TeleClasses

The One Business Page Plan® is available to your company or organization as a workshop, annual retreat, teleclass or complete planning program. Experienced facilitators will tailor the presentation to meet your needs.

All classes and programs are hands-on working sessions designed to teach participants how to write a clear, concise, understandable business plan, on a single page, in the quickest and simplest way possible.

---

## Enterprise Planning Software

This innovative system uniquely links The One Page Business Plan® with an Executive Dashboard and a Simplified Project Tracking System that can be used in a variety of companies from small professional service firms to international corporations.

The system requires no IT support and can be learned in 30 minutes. Interested? The One Page Planning and Performance System is rapidly becoming the planning system of choice for CEOs and business owners.

---

## Professional Certification

We are interested in partnering with experienced business, government, and not-for-profit consultants and coaches. If your firm provides strategic planning and/or performance management consulting services, The One Page Business Plan® may be a profitable addition to your toolkit.

Coaches and consultants who successfully complete the training and certification programs will be licensed to market and deliver One Page Business Plan® products and services.

The One Page Business
Plan® Company
1798 Fifth Street
Berkeley, CA 94710
Phone: (510) 705-8400
Fax: (510) 705-8403
jhoran@onepagebusinessplan.com
www.onepagebusinessplan.com

# The Entrepreneur's CD Toolkit
# How Install and Use the CD

## Installation Instructions:
Simply load the CD into your CD drive. It contains an automatic installer that will create a directory on your hard drive called Entrepreneur's Toolkit CD located in your Program Files Folder.

This CD-ROM is NOT a stand-alone software program and requires the use of Microsoft Word® and/or Excel® to use the templates, forms and spreadsheets.

### If for some reason the auto-installer does not work:
1) Double-click on My Computer
2) Double-click the icon for the CD-ROM
3) Double-click on launch_toolkit.exe

## How to Use Entrepreneur's Toolkit
Click on Toolkit icon on Desktop to open the CD's directory. Directory will contain the following folders:

1. Forms and Templates
2. Sales Calculators
3. Budget Worksheets
4. Scorecards
5. Sample Plans
6. Bonus Tools

Open any folder with a click. Select the desired tool, Word® document or Excel® spreadsheet.

## CAUTION:
Immediately after opening any of the files we encourage you to save the file with a new name using the "SAVE AS" command in order to preserve the original content of the file.

## No Technical Support
This CD is provided without technical or software support. Please refer to your Microsoft Word® or Excel® User Manuals for questions related to the use of these software programs.

## System Requirements:
Windows 95/98/NT/2000/XP
Macintosh OS 9.1 or higher
Microsoft Word® and Excel®
CD/ROM drive
7MB available disk space on hard drive

---

**SOFTWARE LICENSE AGREEMENT**

This is a legal agreement between you, the user, and The One Page Business Plan Company. This agreement covers the software that is distributed with this CD and any subsequent software that may be distributed to you from The One Page Business Plan Company in the form of additional CD's or the Internet.

By opening or breaking the seal on the Software packet(s), installing or downloading the Software, you agree to be bound by the terms of this agreement. If you do not agree to these terms, promptly return the this book and software to the place of purchase.

You may use one copy of the Software on only one computer at a time. If you have multiple licenses for the Software, you may use as many copies at any time as you have licenses. "Use" means loading the Software in temporary memory or permanent storage on the computer. Installation on a network server solely for distribution to other computers is not "use" if (but only if) you have a separate license for each computer to which the Software is distributed. You must ensure that the number of persons using the Software installed on a network server does not exceed the number of licenses that you have. If the number of users of Software installed on a network server will exceed the number of licenses, you must purchase additional licenses until the number of licenses equals the number of users before allowing additional users to use the Software.

**LIMITED WARRANTY**

The One Page Business Plan Company warrants that the Software disks will be free from defects in materials and workmanship under normal use for ninety (90) days from the date you receive them. This warranty is limited to you and is not transferable. Any implied warranties are limited to ninety (90) days from the date you receive the Software. Some jurisdictions do not allow limits on the duration of an implied warranty, so this limitation may not apply to you. The entire liability of The One Page Business Plan Company and its suppliers, and your exclusive remedy, shall be (a) return of the price paid for the Software or (b) replacement of any disk not meeting this warranty. This limited warranty is void if any disk damage has resulted from accident, abuse, or misapplication. Any replacement disk is warranted for the remaining original warranty period or thirty (30) days, whichever is longer.

The One Page Business Plan Company does NOT warrant that the functions of the Software will meet your requirements or that operation of the Software will be uninterrupted or error free. You assume responsibility for selecting the Software to achieve your intended results and for the use and results obtained from the Software.

The Software is protected by United States copyright laws and international treaties. You may make one copy of the Software solely for backup or archival purposes or transfer it to a single hard disk provided you keep the original solely for backup or archival purposes. You may not rent or lease the Software or copy the written materials accompanying the Software, but you may transfer the Software and all accompanying materials on a permanent basis if you retain no copies and the recipient agrees to the terms hereof.

THE ONE PAGE BUSINESS PLAN COMPANY DISCLAIMS ALL OTHER WARRANTIES, EXPRESS OR IMPLIED, INCLUDING, BUT NOT LIMITED TO, IMPLIED WARRANTIES OF MERCHANTABILITY AND FITNESS FOR A PARTICULAR PURPOSE, FOR THE SOFTWARE AND ALL ACCOMPANYING WRITTEN MATERIALS.

This limited warranty gives you specific legal rights; you may have others, which vary from jurisdiction to jurisdiction.

IN NO EVENT SHALL THE ONE PAGE BUSINESS PLAN COMPANY OR ITS SUPPLIERS BE LIABLE FOR ANY DAMAGES WHATSOEVER (INCLUDING, WITHOUT LIMITATION, DAMAGES FOR LOSS OF BUSINESS PROFITS, BUSINESS INTERRUPTION, LOSS OF BUSINESS INFORMATION, OR OTHER PECUNIARY LOSS) ARISING OUT OF USE OR INABILITY TO USE THE SOFTWARE, EVEN IF ADVISED OF THE POSSIBILITY OF SUCH DAMAGES.

Because some jurisdictions do not allow an exclusion or limitation of liability for consequential or incidental damages, the above limitation may not apply to you.